The
Nutshell
Technique

The

Nutshell

Technique

CRACK *the* SECRET *of*
SUCCESSFUL SCREENWRITING

By Jill Chamberlain

FOREWORD *by* PATRICK WRIGHT

University of Texas Press ⟿ Austin

Requests for permission to reproduce material from this work should be sent to:

Permissions
University of Texas Press
P.O. Box 7819
Austin, TX 78713-7819
utpress.utexas.edu/rp-form

♾ The paper used in this book meets the minimum requirements of
ANSI/NISO Z39.48-1992 (R1997) (Permanence of Paper).

Library of Congress Cataloging-in-Publication Data
Chamberlain, Jill, author.
The nutshell technique : crack the secret of successful screenwriting /
by Jill Chamberlain; foreword by Patrick Wright. — First edition.
pages   cm
Includes bibliographical references and index.
ISBN 978-1-4773-0373-3 (pbk. : alk. paper) — ISBN 978-1-4773-0865-3 (library e-book) —
ISBN 978-1-4773-0866-0 (nonlibrary e-book)
1. Motion picture authorship.   2. Motion picture plays—Technique.   I. Title.
PN1996.C49   2016
808.2′3—dc23
2015029017

doi:10.7560/303733

*For my father, who instilled in me
my lifelong love of movies, and my mother,
who always knew I was a writer.*

I could be bounded in a nutshell,
And count myself a king of infinite space.

Hamlet (II, ii, 234–235)

CONTENTS

A NOTE ON THE TEXT

FOR THE SINGULAR THIRD-PERSON PRONOUN, I have opted not to use the archaic "he," "him," and "his"; the tedious "he or she," "him or her," and "his or hers"; and other ungainly options. Instead I have chosen what is often referred to as the "singular they"; that is, using "they," "them," or "their" as a gender-neutral singular third-person pronoun. This usage has become increasingly acceptable in contemporary times, although it has been in use since at least the fourteenth century. Once again, I'll quote Mr. Shakespeare:

> There's not a man I meet but doth salute me
> As if I were their well-acquainted friend.
> **Comedy of Errors (IV, iii, 1–2)**

FOREWORD

JUST OVER A CENTURY AFTER the invention of the moving picture, Jill Chamberlain may be the one to have finally cracked cinema's genetic code.

Jill reveals that there is something deeper at work in successful feature film screenplays, something more than simply three acts and an Inciting Incident. Working behind the scenes (so to speak) are specific dynamics required for creating fully dimensional protagonists and emotionally satisfying stories. Jill has mapped out these key dynamics and calls her method the Nutshell Technique. I am not aware of any other book or method demonstrating anything like it.

Jill positions her method against other approaches, arguing that they are not adequate in explaining the true reasons a feature film screenplay succeeds. She is correct, particularly regarding the canonical works by Robert McKee and Syd Field. While important, these titans fail to bring us to the "soul" of a film.

In general, there are two approaches to screenplay story structure. One focuses on plot. The other focuses on character arc and internal journey. Jill reveals that, in the best screenplays, these two pieces are, in fact, inextricably fused together.

I stress with my students that a protagonist's internal journey should be expressed in the external world of the film. Every choice the filmmaker makes—regarding, for example, mise-en-scène, pacing, or lighting—should relate to the inner conflict of the film's lead character. The darkness and decay of Gotham City mirrors Batman's inner struggle to direct his rage and pain toward justice instead of vengeance.

This book presents a holistic and systematic view of why certain film screenplays work better than others. To explain the Nutshell Technique, Jill applies it to thirty well-known films, demonstrating just how stakes are set up and propel the story forward. Reading through her film examples is something of a revelation. Suddenly you see why the Climax in great dramatic films can produce the adrenaline rush you would expect from an action picture. And then you realize that some action pictures are deeper than they may at first appear, resonating with us long after their 120 minutes on the screen have ended and entreating us to reconsider humankind's biggest philosophical questions. It dawns on the reader why there is such a large graveyard of failed "blockbusters," and why this didn't have to be.

There comes a point in developing almost any screenplay when you cannot see the forest for the trees and you lose perspective. The Nutshell Technique gives you back perspective. In requiring writers to identify story elements at their most essential, the Nutshell Technique guides them toward finding the authentic story that they originally intended to tell.

As screenwriters, we need better tools to help us develop more resonant stories. As educators, we need tools that help our students understand the mechanisms at work in great storytelling. In these pages, Jill Chamberlain has put together a fantastic tool set. Cinephiles will also find this book insightful, because it is filled with excellent examples of films that succeed due to Nutshell Technique mechanisms working behind the scenes.

This book is truly a must-read for anyone at all serious about understanding the mystery behind what makes a successful screenplay work.

Patrick Wright

Director, MFA in Filmmaking, Maryland Institute College
of Art, and Co-Director, Johns Hopkins University and
Maryland Institute College of Art Film Center

ACKNOWLEDGMENTS

I don't think I could thank Gianna LaMorte enough. She championed the Nutshell Technique, and me, and made this book possible.

For suffering early drafts and patiently and kindly offering improvements, my deepest thanks to Nancy Foley, Tracie Gardner, Lynne Chapman, Sue Carter, and my editor, Jim Burr.

Leigh Newsom did an amazing job of transforming the Nutshell Technique form from the crude Word document I had been using into the dynamic schematic you see in these pages, and I'm truly thankful for his artistry.

For lending their professional expertise, sincerest thanks to Robin Weinburgh, Carson Coots, Keith Jaasma, Erik Ruvalcaba, Mirna Hariz, Jinni Fontana, and Sherry Mills.

I had wonderful teachers back in the day, most especially Doug Katz, who instilled in me my love and respect for the craft of screenwriting, and my first film professor, the late Stefan Sharff, who forever changed how I watch movies.

My thanks to a number of writers who helped me with the film Nutshells: Andrew Olson, Jordan Buckley, Dewey Badeaux, Tony Vu, Simon Renwick, Laura Menghini, and Tomas Burke.

And last but certainly not least, thank you to all the screenwriters I work with in my workshops and in private consultation. You continue to surprise and amaze me with the seemingly infinite possibilities you find for your wonderfully original stories—despite my hardheaded insistence that you incorporate these eight elements—and you show me every day that technique alone accomplishes nothing without imagination.

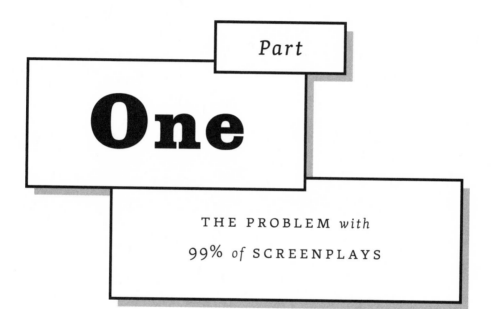

Part

One

THE PROBLEM *with*
99% *of* SCREENPLAYS

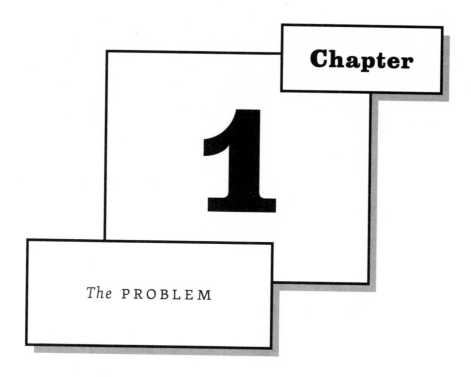

Chapter

1

The PROBLEM

Why Another Screenwriting Method?

AS A SCREENPLAY CONSULTANT and screenwriting instructor, I can tell you firsthand that 99% of amateur screenwriters fail to tell a story.

These writers may know how to properly format a script, how to write snappy dialogue, and how to set the scenes. They may have an interesting character here and there and perhaps some clever plot devices. But, invariably, while they may have the kernel of a good idea for a screenplay, they fail to tell a *story* that works. What the 99% present instead is a *situation*.

The solution lies in story structure. A misunderstood and often poorly conveyed subject, story structure is both the most difficult and the most important concept in screenwriting, accounting for about 75% of the screenwriter's creative effort.

There is a central unifying system at work behind great screenplays. It consists of eight requisite elements and, most importantly, essential *interdependencies* between these elements.

I needed a straightforward way to convey to my clients and students what was not working structurally in their screenplays, and I wanted a road map to show them exactly how to fix things. I mapped out these eight elements and their interdependencies and put it all on a one-page form. I somewhat glibly labeled that first piece of paper "Screenplay in a Nutshell," and this approach became known as the **Nutshell Technique**.

This dynamic system is the hidden structure behind the greatest screenplays. You'll find it working behind the scenes in *Casablanca*, *Chinatown*, *The Godfather*, and *Pulp Fiction*. Consciously or not, screenwriters including Charlie Kaufman, Michael Arndt, and Diablo Cody all incorporate its principles.

There are people in Hollywood who are said to "intuitively" know story. What I'm doing is giving you a huge shortcut to story intuition.

I hear some screenwriting theorists say their approaches are "descriptive, not prescriptive." Well, in my workshops, the Nutshell Technique is prescriptive. Writers use it up front as a worksheet to get straight to the guts of their story and make sure it works before they've even started a screenplay or treatment. They identify the Nutshell Technique's eight elements in their own story, and the Nutshell Technique form gives them a visual means to check whether or not the essential interdependencies are working together correctly. If the elements are all working, the writer knows that they have the basis for a structurally solid story. If the elements are not all working together, the writer knows they have a situation instead of a story, and they can see right on the form their options for how to transform their situation into a story that works.

The Nutshell Technique doesn't make stories more alike or formulaic. It makes them better and more powerful. It pushes writers to find less predictable directions for their stories, making them more satisfying. Writers who use the Nutshell Technique find that figuring out this little bit of structure—just eight things—frees them instead of restricting them. Setting up a sound structure from the get-go allows writers to write truthfully and without inhibition. The Nutshell Technique helps guide them to tell the story they originally intended to tell.

[4]

You'll see the Nutshell Technique structure behind the vast majority of feature films released in the United States. Almost all will contain a version of these eight elements. The Nutshell Technique interdependencies may not be working in the films 100% of the time, but often I find that had the story been tweaked so all eight elements *did* work, it seems it would have been a better movie.

This is not a comprehensive how-to book on screenwriting. Subjects such as screenplay formatting, dialogue, and character development are outside of its scope. The focus here is on something more essential and so often misunderstood: how to structure a screenplay so that it tells a compelling, satisfying story.

Learn the Nutshell Technique and you'll have an incredibly powerful tool for harnessing the full potential that a well-crafted tale can have.

The Traditional Three-Act Screenplay

Since the existence of the first feature-length films at the beginning of the twentieth century, Hollywood has structured screenplays in three acts. The first book explaining the three-act screenplay model, however, wouldn't come until 1979 when the late Syd Field published *Screenplay*.

Today most screenwriting theorists continue to incorporate the three-act paradigm (a few claim a different number of acts, but it seems to me those theorists are parsing the same three acts). I also begin with the three-act model, although it alone isn't enough to ensure that a story is structurally sound. But it functions as the most basic foundation for the screenplay. So let me review.

THE GENERALLY AGREED-UPON PRINCIPLES OF FEATURE-SCREENPLAY THREE-ACT STRUCTURE

Most feature-length films are about two hours long or a little under, usually around 110 to 120 minutes. Most screenplays are between 110 and 120 pages. This is not a coincidence. One of the reasons the film industry has stuck with the odd margins and the antiquated Courier font from back when screenplays were written on typewriters is because someone realized early on that one page of a formatted screenplay is roughly equal to one minute of screen time. I'll be referring to pages and minutes largely interchangeably because they essentially are the same in screenwriting.

[5]

In the three-act screenplay, Act 1 is about 30 pages; Act 2 is twice as long, about 60 pages; and Act 3 is about 30 pages.

Act 1 introduces us to the protagonist and their world, and at around page 25, there is a turning point that will spin the story in a different direction. There are a lot of different terms used for this turning point but most everyone agrees every feature-film screenplay needs a strong event to push the story and the protagonist into the figurative New World that is Act 2. Field called it Plot Point 1, and so we'll call it that for now.

It is often said that the story *really* begins with Act 2. The protagonist's life has been pushed in a previously unexpected direction and now, as many a clichéd film synopsis says, "complications ensue." In Act 2, the protagonist will face a seemingly unending series of obstacles.

Act 2 ends in another turning point that will move the story in yet another direction, usually at around pages 85 to 90. Field called this turning point Plot Point 2. It pushes the story and the protagonist into Act 3, which is known as the Resolution. At the very beginning of Act 3 is what most screenwriters would define as the Climax of the story, which is also sometimes known as the False Resolution. By the end of Act 3 the story is fully resolved.

The vast majority of books on screenwriting structure present the three-act approach. From here, the existing books typically fall into one of three camps when it comes to further discussion of screenplay structure:

- Like Field, they lay out only the bare minimum requirements of three-act structure and leave you hanging when it comes to how to develop a plot into a satisfying story. Writers who try to use these approaches usually find themselves petering out by the beginning of Act 2, as their plots lose tension and organic conflict.
- Some give advice and present theories that are all over the place with no unified central principles. They just point out a bunch of different little observations of elements that may hold true in *Casablanca* or *Chinatown* but may very well not be true for the story you are trying to tell. Writers trying to use these approaches, having been given no coherent structure, often never even get started.
- Others give you a one-size-fits-all, paint-by-numbers Hollywood movie

boilerplate, dictating some 12 or 15 or 22 required moments. As you might expect, these scripts tend to tell similar tales. And while these 12 to 22 steps may hold true for *Star Wars*, many great films clearly do not follow them. Some writers using these approaches will realize how unsatisfying their screenplays are to write, and thus to read, and will abandon them. Other writers will actually get to the end of their screenplays, and then are puzzled as to why they can't break into Hollywood with them. They will continue to write unsatisfying screenplay after unsatisfying screenplay, never gaining insight into why things are going wrong.

And here's the thing: you can follow the advice of all three camps and still fail to tell a story, which is what 99% of amateur screenwriters end up doing.

None of the books explain the *interdependencies* between key elements that are spread out over the three acts and specific *intersections* that occur between the plot and the protagonist's character arc. These interrelationships and intersections are required to properly tell a story.

Comedy and Tragedy

Syd Field didn't do this, but other screenwriting instructors, myself included, find it useful to divide all feature-film screenplays into two categories: comedies and tragedies.

When we speak of comedies in this context, we're not talking about the film genre of comedy. We're using the academic definitions of comedy and tragedy as described by Aristotle in his work *Poetics* over 2,300 years ago. As a matter of fact, thousands of books have been written on screenwriting, and as a sum total they have added about 5% to the understanding of dramatic storytelling that was first laid out by Aristotle over 2,200 years before the invention of the motion picture.

In a tragedy, Aristotle said, the protagonist has a change of fortune that

must be not to good fortune from bad but, on the contrary, from good to bad fortune, and it must not be due to villainy but to some great flaw in such a man.[1]

Applied to the feature-film screenplay:

> A **tragedy** is a story where the protagonist fails to overcome a flaw and falls from good fortune to bad, which means it usually has a sad ending.

A comedy is essentially the opposite.[2] In a feature-film screenplay:

> A **comedy** is a story where the protagonist is able to overcome their flaw and learn its opposite, and the protagonist sees their fortune go from bad to good, which means it usually has a happy ending.

Story versus Situation

As I noted previously, 99% of amateur screenwriters fail to tell a *story*. Instead, their screenplays present a *situation*. What I call situational, Aristotle called episodic:

> Of "simple" plots and actions the worst are those which are "episodic." By this I mean a plot in which the episodes do not follow each other probably or inevitably.[3]

In the better stories, Aristotle said,

> Such events do not seem to be mere accidents. So such plots as these must necessarily be the best.[4]

A great character, it has been said, is a story waiting to happen. A story should be unique to its protagonist. The events of the story should uniquely test traits specific to the protagonist.

If I can take your protagonist out and replace them with a completely different character, and with a few tweaks make your script work just as well with this new protagonist, your script is presenting a situation and is not truly a story.

Let's say we took that timeless classic *Groundhog Day* and, instead of Phil the weatherman (Bill Murray) being the protagonist, we made his producer Rita (played by Andie MacDowell) the protagonist. To remind you of the character: she's new at their Pittsburgh TV station, and she's good-natured and guileless, perhaps a little naive. And the second day in Punxsutawney we'll make *her* be the one who wakes up and discovers it's Groundhog Day again. When she meets up with Phil, he hasn't experienced this. Phil and everybody else in Punxsutawney are experiencing this day for the first time. Rita, our new protagonist, is the only one experiencing the phenomenon of the day repeating itself. Our script will follow her as she finds herself trapped, repeating Groundhog Day indefinitely and trying to find a way to make it stop.

Can you imagine this version? We'll call it, to distinguish it from the original, *Rita's Groundhog Day*. What do you think? Would it be as good as the original *Groundhog Day*?

It would almost work. It relies on an excellent premise: what if someone had to experience the same day over and over, indefinitely? That alone is a fascinating concept ripe with potential. But it's not a story. And making Rita the protagonist at the center of that premise still doesn't make it a story. *Rita's Groundhog Day* would be a situation, not a story.

> 99% of amateur screenplays are akin to *Rita's Groundhog Day*—they present a situation and not a story.

And a good percentage of professional screenplays do, too. So what's the difference? What makes the original *Groundhog Day* truly a story while *Rita's Groundhog Day* is merely a situation?

The difference is *Rita's Groundhog Day* has a great plot device but the wrong protagonist. It's no accident that Phil the weatherman is the protagonist of the real *Groundhog Day*.

The screenwriters deliberately created a protagonist whose central flaw is that he's egocentric. The central conceit of the film, that the day won't move forward, is a great test, perhaps the perfect test, of someone who is egocentric. Having to live the same day over and over is going to force him, eventually, to change. Thinking only of himself eventually grows tiresome. Over time he discovers the only way to bring meaning to his life, as he has to repeat the same day, is to do for others. By the end he has changed 180 degrees from being egocentric to caring about others, and the Universe finally releases him and lets February 3 come. *That* is a story.

Rita's Groundhog Day isn't a story. We'd be relying on a clever premise but without a protagonist with the right flaw, it's a totally arbitrary situation we're putting her into. If I had to identify a flaw for Rita, I'd say she's a bit naive. Having a plot that centers on the same day repeating indefinitely isn't a good fit for a protagonist whose flaw is naiveté. In an Aristotelian comedy, we see the protagonist change from their central flaw and learn the opposite in the end. If Rita is our protagonist, we'd want her to learn the opposite of naiveté: wisdom. I don't see her being able to gain wisdom from the monotony of living the day over and over. If she is repeating the same day, she's going to quickly figure the ins and outs of everything going on around her. Her naiveté won't be tested. For her to find wisdom, Rita would be better served by a plot that challenged her naiveté, something that would force her to not take things at face value. Instead of waking up and repeating the same day in the same place, it would be a closer fit for her character to have a plot where she woke up and found herself in a completely different place and maybe even a different time period every morning. *That* might force her to challenge her own naiveté.

[10] Let me give you another example. Let's take *Tootsie*. I'm going to keep the same protagonist, Michael Dorsey, the out-of-work actor played by Dustin Hoffman. But this time I'm going to change the plot a little. Instead

of having him disguise himself as a woman and audition for the part of a female character on a soap opera, I'm going to have him audition for a male part, but it's going to be a part that is specifically an extremely overweight man. He's going to have a makeup artist friend create prosthetics, padding, and makeup so he looks like he weighs 300 pounds.

Michael is going to audition disguised as an obese man, and he's going to get the part. I'm going to keep the rest of the plot the same. He's going to get a crush on his co-star Julie, and they are going to become close friends. He'll tell her he's gay, so she doesn't perceive any sexual tension between them. But the rest of the plot can stay the same. He's going to be rushing around, getting in and out of his fat suit and makeup, comically struggling to keep his identity a secret. Eventually he'll grow to hate doing it so much that at the Climax, live on the air, he'll pull the prosthetics off of his face and reveal the padding under his clothing. To distinguish it from the original, we'll call it *Big Tootsie*.

So how well would *Big Tootsie* work? Both *Tootsie* and *Big Tootsie* deal with a secret identity, which tends to make for great comedy. A man running around pretending to be a woman is often funny. Similarly, a small man pretending to be a big man could be funny. But *Big Tootsie* would fail to tell a story.

> 99% of amateur screenplays amount to *Big Tootsie*—they present a situation, not a story.

With *Big Tootsie*, this time we have the right protagonist but the wrong plot. Among Michael's flaws in the original *Tootsie* is that he doesn't respect women. Making him have to pretend to be a woman is the perfect test of this flaw. *That's* what makes it a great story. With *Big Tootsie*, instead of a story, we've put Michael Dorsey in a totally arbitrary situation. Having to pretend to be fat is a plot device that has nothing to do with the Michael Dorsey character. Now, if we changed the character and gave him a bias against overweight people, *Big Tootsie* could potentially work. Having to pretend to be overweight would be a good test of someone who looks down on overweight people.

Identifying a central flaw in your protagonist is an essential component of screenplay story structure. While some of the other books on this subject may talk about the importance of a central flaw, none I know of show you how this part of your protagonist's character arc must intersect with specific points in your plot in order for your story to work like a story and not be merely a situation.

> If you miss these critical intersections, you will end up in the 99% with *Rita's Groundhog Day* or *Big Tootsie*: a situation instead of a story.

Reversals

The other very common problem I see screenwriters have is they miss the opportunity to take their protagonist far enough. They fail to take the protagonist, and the reader, on a truly profound journey because they overlook opportunities in a story for the protagonist to go through reversals. It was Aristotle who said that the best plots contain reversals, which he defined as "a change of the situation into the opposite."[5]

Aristotle divided dramatic plays into two parts: the Complication, which is everything from the beginning of the play until the beginning of a change of fortune, and the Denouement, or Resolution, which is from the beginning of the change of fortune to the end of the play.[6] It's very similar to our contemporary three acts. If we just combine our Act 1 and Act 2, it's the equivalent of Aristotle's Complication (remember: our Act 2 is described as "complications ensue"). And our Act 3 is also known as the Resolution.

Great films have one or two major reversals. If they are Aristotelian comedies, they have two. In tragedies, the protagonist fails to achieve the first reversal, which leads to a different reversal occurring: one from good fortune to bad. I'm going to go through the two reversals that are in Aristotelian comedies first, and then I'll discuss the reversal and the failure to achieve another reversal that occur in tragedies.

> The majority of amateur screenplays miss the opportunity to show their protagonist undergo the profound reversal(s) that great stories reveal.

Great films that are Aristotelian comedies show their protagonists going through two profound reversals, which happen at specific points in the running time that correlate to Aristotle's division of the story into Complication and Resolution. Like Aristotle's Complication, the first reversal starts with the protagonist's very first scene and ends with the beginning of a change of fortune at the end of Act 2. In a feature film, this beginning of a change of fortune is at a turning point that Syd Field called Plot Point 2, at around the 75% point in the running time.

In this reversal, the protagonist will go from wanting to achieve one specific goal in their first scene to the exact opposite state of mind or situation at their lowest point at close to 75% into the running time. For example:

- In *The Godfather* (which, yes, is an Aristotelian comedy in academic terms), in Michael Corleone's first scene he says he's not his father and he's not going to get into the family business. What's happening at 77% into the running time? He's made a complete reversal: Don Vito Corleone names Michael head of the family.
- In *Pulp Fiction*, Jules (Samuel L. Jackson) in his first scene wants to prevent his boss Marsellus from being "fucked like a bitch." Guess what's happening at 68% into the running time? That's right: that's when Marsellus is being raped by Zed.

Marsellus (Ving Rhames) right before he's raped near the 75% point in the film's running time. This is a complete reversal—the exact opposite—of what protagonist Jules (Samuel L. Jackson) wanted in his first scene. Still from *Pulp Fiction*. Copyright 1994, Miramax Films.

Great films that are Aristotelian comedies see their protagonists go through a second profound reversal. Like Aristotle's Resolution, the second reversal starts at the beginning of the change of fortune for the protagonist (where the first reversal ended, at around 75% into the running time), and it ends in their last scene.

In an Aristotelian comedy, this change of fortune takes the protagonist from their lowest point at around 75% in the running time to their usually happy ending in the very end. Simultaneous to their reversal of fortune from bad to good, the protagonist changes and makes a personal reversal from their central flaw to its polar opposite: the personal strength they learn in the end. For example:

- In *Frozen*, Anna, the younger sister, has the central flaw of being selfish. At her lowest point, 83% into the running time, her older sister Elsa is about to be killed and Anna is about to be frozen to death. She chooses to try to save Elsa's life instead of letting herself be saved. In her final scene she gives Kristoff a replacement sled. In the end she has made a 180-degree change from selfishness to selflessness.

While there are two profound reversals in great films that are Aristotelian comedies, in tragedies, the protagonist fails to achieve the first reversal, and that leads to their final reversal: from good fortune to bad.

Instead of experiencing a first reversal and failing to achieve their goal, like they would in an Aristotelian comedy, in a tragedy, the protagonist not only achieves their initial goal, they surpass it by the beginning of a change of fortune. This beginning of a change of fortune is at what Field called Plot Point 2, at around 75% into the running time. Instead of this being their lowest moment, like it is in an Aristotelian comedy, it is their highest moment of success. For example:

- In the first scene of *The Social Network*, protagonist Mark Zuckerberg wants to get into a club. At his highest point, at 84% into the running time, he's the CEO of a club with a million members.

In great films that are tragedies, the protagonist ends up on top at around 75% into the running time. They have achieved their goal and then some. But this 75% point also marks a turning point that is the beginning of a change of fortune. Aristotle said that this change of fortune in a tragedy is from good to bad and is brought about due to the protagonist's flaw. For example:

- At exactly 75% in the running time in *Sunset Blvd.*, hack screenwriter Joe Gillis is at his happiest moment and point of greatest achievement. He and Betty are writing a script, one with depth and meaning, and they are in love. Norma calls Betty, hinting at Norma and Joe's relationship. Betty gives Joe excuses and tells him she never heard any of it. But Joe's flaw of cynicism overtakes him, and he cruelly forces Betty to hear the whole truth about his sordid situation, driving her away. As Joe packs to leave Norma, he reveals the ugly truth that her servant has been writing the fan letters she thinks she's been getting from the public, and Norma shoots Joe dead.

For the tragic ending to feel satisfying, the tragic protagonist can't have had all bad luck. Their reversal of fortune from good to bad should be brought on mostly due to their own flaw. Likewise in an Aristotelian comedy, the protagonist should see their reversal of fortune in the Resolution go from bad to good largely due to their change from having a central, personal flaw to its opposite.

[15]

Reversals are a powerful dramatic tool, which is why great screenplays have them.

So now that we've addressed the foundations of story and the general types of changes protagonists should undergo and when, it's time to carry Aristotle's wisdom forward to the present.

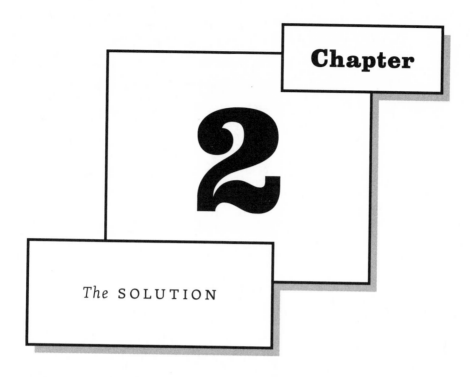

Chapter

2

The SOLUTION

The Nutshell Technique: A New Paradigm

FOR THE SCREENWRITERS I WORK WITH in my workshops and in consultations, I created the Nutshell Technique form. It's a worksheet in the form of a schematic that asks writers to identify their protagonist and eight essential story elements that should be in their screenplays. The schematic allows them to see all the elements on one page and, most importantly, enables them to verify visually that the elements' key interdependencies are working together correctly. If the interdependencies work together correctly, it means they have eliminated from their story the chronic problems I see in 99% of amateur screenplays.

The Nutshell Technique depicts the story at its most essential. Almost all great screenplays have these elements and their requisite interdependencies (although not every screenplay that has them is necessarily great).

I'll explain in detail the relationships among the eight elements in upcoming chapters. In the text of this book, I will indicate each of the eight key story elements in all capital letters, such as the FLAW. The last section of the book, Part 4, "Film Nutshells," consists of Nutshell Technique forms filled out for 30 famous and otherwise noteworthy films, in alphabetical order by title. When in the text of this book I discuss a specific film's Nutshell element that is cross-referenced in Part 4 and quoted verbatim, I will underline this text (e.g., Michael Corleone's FLAW is naiveté). When this happens, you may want to flip to Part 4, find the film title's Nutshell Technique form, and see how the Nutshell element fits dynamically into the whole Nutshell Technique structure. If I discuss theoretical or incorrectly stated Nutshell elements, I'll indicate those inside of quotation marks (e.g., Juno's SET-UP WANT might be "to figure out what to do").

There are two different schematics: one for Aristotelian comedies and another for tragedies. The Nutshell Technique form for Aristotelian comedy is shown on the following page.

Here, in brief, is how the Nutshell Technique works in an Aristotelian comedy:

In their first dialogue scene, the protagonist will establish their SET-UP WANT. Protagonists have multiple things they want, but the SET-UP WANT is specifically something they want that they'll get in the POINT OF NO RETURN, which is the term I use for what Syd Field called Plot Point 1, the event that pushes the protagonist into Act 2 and spins the story in a new direction.

The POINT OF NO RETURN brings the protagonist something they wanted, their first-scene SET-UP WANT, along with something they didn't want, the CATCH. The CATCH is the perfect test of the protagonist's FLAW.

The POINT OF NO RETURN should happen and the impact of its CATCH be felt all by 25% into the film's total running time or the script's page count (by 0:30:00 in a 120-minute film or by page 30 of a 120-page screenplay).

In Act 2 of an Aristotelian comedy, the protagonist will find their fortune falling lower and lower until they reach their lowest point at about 75% into the running time or the script's page count (by 1:30:00 in a 120-minute film or page 90 of a 120-page screenplay). Syd Field called this moment Plot Point 2. Because this moment is their lowest point in a comedy, the term I use is the CRISIS. It is both the protagonist's lowest point and the exact opposite position or situation from where the protagonist hoped to be in their first-scene SET-UP WANT.

As they begin Act 3, the protagonist will make a big decision, the

Nutshell Technique form for comedy

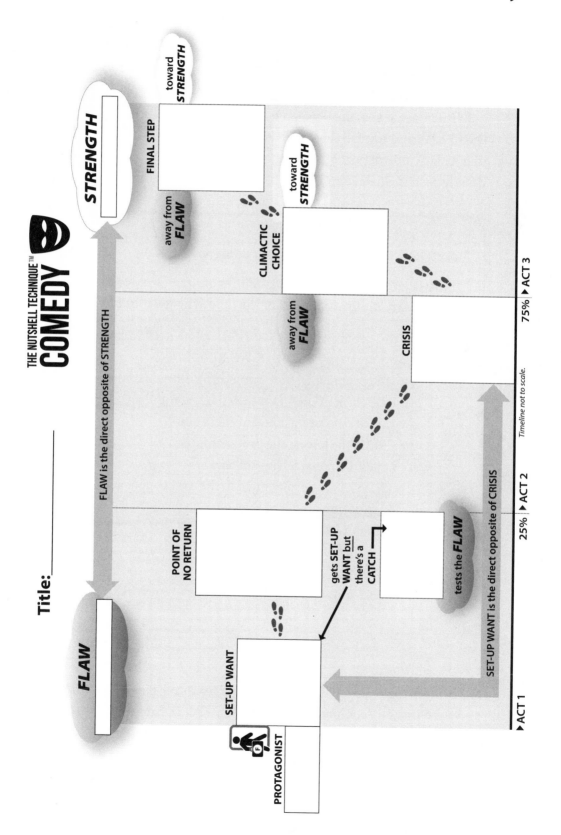

CLIMACTIC CHOICE. In an Aristotelian comedy, the CLIMACTIC CHOICE is a step the protagonist makes away from their FLAW and toward its opposite, the STRENGTH. This is a step in a positive direction but it's not enough to bring the comedic protagonist a happy ending, yet.

In their last scene, the protagonist will make another move away from their FLAW and toward their STRENGTH in their FINAL STEP. This move in a positive direction often brings the protagonist the happy ending usually seen in an Aristotelian comedy.

Nutshell Technique Checklist: Comedy

Here is a checklist for the Nutshell Technique form for comedy. To properly set up a story, all of the following must be true:

☐ Does the protagonist get their SET-UP WANT immediately and directly in the POINT OF NO RETURN?

☐ Does the protagonist get something immediately in the POINT OF NO RETURN that they don't want, the CATCH?

☐ Is the CATCH the perfect test of their FLAW?

☐ Is the CRISIS the lowest the protagonist can go? (What if they were in jail? Or considering suicide?)

☐ In the CRISIS, is the protagonist in the exact opposite state of mind or situation of where they were in the SET-UP WANT?

☐ In both the CLIMACTIC CHOICE and the FINAL STEP, does the protagonist move away from the FLAW and toward the STRENGTH?

☐ Are the FLAW and the STRENGTH exact opposites?

Here's how the Nutshell Technique works for *Silver Linings Playbook* (see also the Nutshell Technique form filled out for it in Part 4):

In his first dialogue scene, protagonist Pat Solatano (Bradley Cooper) is in his room at a psychiatric facility, and he reads out loud a letter he is writing to his estranged wife. He blew it before, he says. He didn't appreciate her. But things are going to be different, he promises. "It's all gonna be better now. I'm better now," he says as he reads his letter. His SET-UP WANT is <u>to be better for his wife</u>.

The POINT OF NO RETURN happens at 0:24:48–0:28:50 (20–24% into the movie's running time), when he is introduced to Tiffany. He blurts out that <u>she looks nice but he's not flirting; he's practicing being better for his wife</u>. Note that in the POINT OF NO RETURN he got exactly what he wanted in his first scene: <u>to be better for his wife</u>. He complimented Tiffany, showing he appreciates her effort to look nice, the way that he needs to treat his wife. He's achieving his WANT <u>to be better for his wife</u> by practicing being attentive with Tiffany.

He gets his first-scene SET-UP WANT in the POINT OF NO RETURN, but in this same timeframe he also gets a CATCH: <u>the woman he is "practicing" on has serious issues</u>. The CATCH isn't something he discovers later but instead, right now. During the POINT OF NO RETURN he notes that she has "poor social skills" and is "mean." This CATCH, that she <u>has serious issues</u>, is going to be the perfect test of his FLAW: he has a <u>lack of control over his emotions</u>.

The POINT OF NO RETURN signals the end of Act 1, and Pat's primary obstacle throughout Act 2 will be the CATCH that Tiffany <u>has serious issues</u> combined with his FLAW of <u>a lack of control over his emotions</u>.

Silver Linings Playbook is an Aristotelian comedy, which means the protagonist will change 180 degrees from their FLAW and learn the opposite, their STRENGTH, and usually will have a happy ending. It also means that at the end of Act 2 the protagonist will reach their CRISIS, which is both their lowest point and the opposite of their SET-UP WANT. Pat reaches his CRISIS at 1:33:04–1:34:29 (76% into the running time). Pat quits as Tiffany's dance partner. She tells him he's failed at being a better man "if it's me reading the signs." This phrase makes him realize Tiffany faked the letter and that she did so because she cares for him, and he <u>no longer cares about being better for his wife</u>. At the CRISIS he is at the direct opposite of how he felt in his first-scene SET-UP WANT: <u>to be better for his wife</u>.

The CLIMACTIC CHOICE in an Aristotelian comedy is a step the protagonist makes away from their FLAW and toward their STRENGTH. When Tiffany is upset to see Pat's wife at the dance contest and starts to get cold feet, he makes the CLIMACTIC CHOICE and <u>insists they go through</u>

with the dance contest. This is moving away from his FLAW of a lack of control over his emotions and toward the STRENGTH of being in control of his emotions. In an Aristotelian comedy, the protagonist will continue to move away from the FLAW and toward the STRENGTH in the FINAL STEP, which is the last major scene of the movie. Pat's FINAL STEP is he runs after Tiffany and gives her the letter he wrote a week earlier saying he loves her. Pat has fully gained the STRENGTH of being in control of his emotions.

The Nutshell Technique form for tragedy is shown on the following page. Here is how the Nutshell Technique works in a tragedy:

In their first dialogue scene, the protagonist will establish their SET-UP WANT. Protagonists have multiple things they want, but the SET-UP WANT is specifically something they want that they'll get in the POINT OF NO RETURN, the event that pushes the protagonist into Act 2 and spins the story in a new direction.

The POINT OF NO RETURN brings the protagonist something they wanted, their first-scene SET-UP WANT, along with something they didn't want, the CATCH. The CATCH is the perfect test of the protagonist's FLAW.

The POINT OF NO RETURN should happen and the impact of its CATCH be felt all by 25% into the film's total running time or the script's page count (by 0:30:00 in a 120-minute film or page 30 of a 120-page screenplay).

In Act 2 of a tragedy, the protagonist will find their fortune rising higher and higher until they reach their highest point at about 75% into the running time or the script's page count (by 1:30:00 in a 120-minute film or page 90 of a 120-page screenplay). Syd Field called this moment Plot Point 2. The term I use when it's a tragedy is the TRIUMPH. It is both the protagonist's highest point and the ultimate manifestation of their first-scene SET-UP WANT.

As they begin Act 3, the protagonist will make a big decision, the CLI-MACTIC CHOICE. In a tragedy, the CLIMACTIC CHOICE is a failure to move toward the STRENGTH and instead is a move that furthers their FLAW. It's a step in a negative direction and will bring the tragic protagonist closer to their typically sad ending.

In their last scene, the FINAL STEP, the protagonist will, again, fail to

[22]

Nutshell Technique form for tragedy

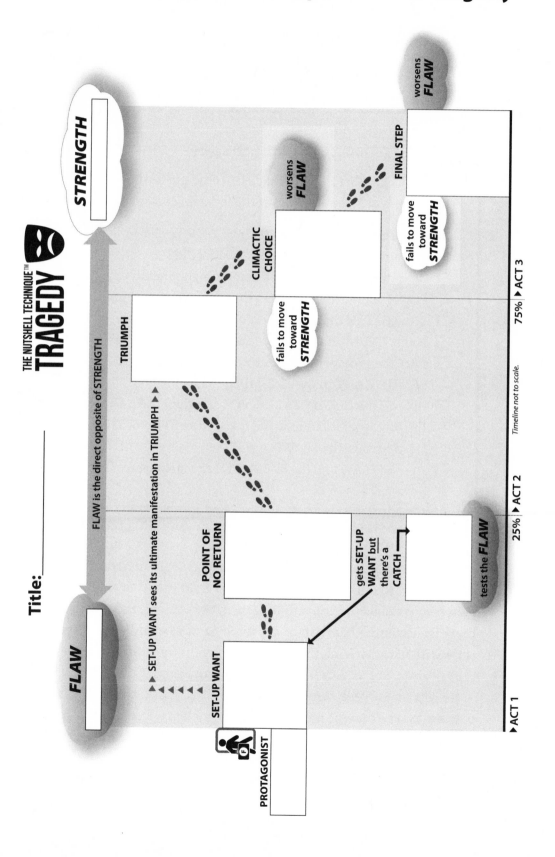

move toward the STRENGTH and instead move even further toward the FLAW. It's another step in a negative direction, sealing the protagonist's fate in what is usually a sad ending.

Nutshell Technique Checklist: Tragedy

Here is a checklist for the Nutshell Technique form for tragedy. To properly set up a story, all of the following must be true:

☐ Does the protagonist get their SET-UP WANT immediately and directly in the POINT OF NO RETURN?
☐ Does the protagonist get something immediately in the POINT OF NO RETURN that they don't want, the CATCH?
☐ Is the CATCH the perfect test of their FLAW?
☐ Is the TRIUMPH the highest the protagonist can go?
☐ Does the protagonist get the ultimate manifestation of their SET-UP WANT in the TRIUMPH?
☐ In both the CLIMACTIC CHOICE and the FINAL STEP, does the protagonist fail to move toward the STRENGTH and instead further the FLAW?
☐ Are the FLAW and the STRENGTH exact opposites?

Here's how the Nutshell Technique works for *The Social Network* (see also the filled-out Nutshell Technique form in Part 4):

In his first dialogue scene, protagonist Mark Zuckerberg (Jesse Eisenberg) is discussing his wish to get into one of Harvard's exclusive final clubs with his girlfriend, Erica, who also breaks up with him in the same conversation. His SET-UP WANT is <u>to get into a final club</u>.

He gets his SET-UP WANT in the POINT OF NO RETURN at 0:22:21–

[24] 0:27:29 (18–23% into the movie's running time): <u>in a final club, he gets the inspiration for Facebook</u>. In the bicycle room of Harvard's most exclusive final club, the Winklevoss twins ask him to program their Harvard social website. Combined with his Facemash idea, it inspires him to create

Facebook. Mark gets his SET-UP WANT <u>to get into a final club</u> literally when he meets the twins in the bicycle room of their final club and figuratively when he hatches a plan to create Facebook. "It's like a final club," he tells his best friend and soon-to-be co-founder Eduardo, "except we're the president." The CATCH is that <u>his idea could be seen as similar to the Winklevosses'</u>. His FLAW is <u>hubris</u>. He thinks his website is beyond comparison with the Winklevosses' idea and that he is such a talented programmer that he can get away with anything.

The Social Network is an Aristotelian tragedy, which means at the end of Act 2 the protagonist will reach their TRIUMPH—their highest point and the ultimate manifestation of their SET-UP WANT. Mark's TRIUMPH is at 1:41:10–1:41:15 (84% into the running time): <u>he's the CEO of his own "final club" with a million members</u> and Facebook celebrates with a party. He has surpassed his SET-UP WANT <u>to get into a final club</u> beyond his wildest dreams.

The CLIMACTIC CHOICE in an Aristotelian tragedy is a failure to move away from the FLAW (<u>hubris</u>) and toward the STRENGTH (<u>humility</u>). Mark's CLIMACTIC CHOICE is <u>he cheats his best friend in the new deal</u>. The FINAL STEP is the last scene of the film and shows a further failure to move away from the FLAW and toward the STRENGTH: <u>he sends his ex-girlfriend</u>—Erica, from the first scene—<u>a Friend Request and hits Refresh over and over</u>, hoping in vain she'll accept it. He fails to gain the STRENGTH of <u>humility</u>.

Your story doesn't have to be predictable to follow these principles. Look at the myriad of movies I've included in Part 4! These dynamic elements don't make stories all the same. They make them *better*. The Nutshell Technique will help you find dramatic weight and meaning where perhaps before there was little or none. It will push you to find directions that are actually *less* predictable. It will ensure that you are telling a story uniquely made for your protagonist, and not merely tossing them into an arbitrary situation.

Part

Two

The NUTSHELL
TECHNIQUE PROCESS

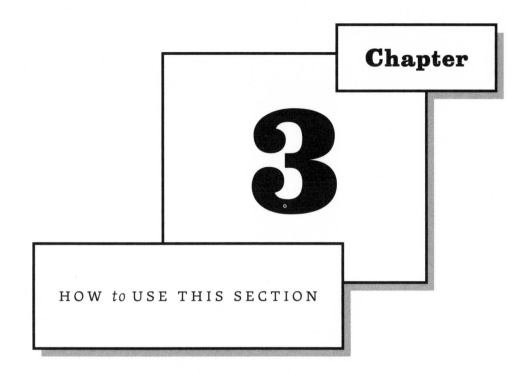

Chapter

3

HOW *to* USE THIS SECTION

LEARNING THE NUTSHELL TECHNIQUE is not easy. It's one thing for me to show how cleverly it works behind the scenes in some famous films. It's quite another to get it to work for the nuances of *your* story.

At the beginning of each chapter going forward, there is a list with the heading "Film Nutshells Discussed in This Chapter." I tried to select films that are well known. You may want to watch or rewatch some of the films as you read the book, and try to Nutshell them; that is, see if you can identify some or all of the eight dynamic Nutshell elements on the Nutshell Technique form. You can flip back to Part 4: Film Nutshells, the last section of the book, where all 30 film Nutshells are in alphabetical order and compare your answers. I will be revealing integral plot elements as needed. So if you haven't seen a film, you may want to skip ahead in the chapter to the next film example until you are able to see the film. Films I mention briefly that are not included in Part 4 are identified as "(not Nutshelled)."

The Nutshell Technique takes practice. In my workshops, I assign a film for my participating writers to view each week, and they try to determine its Nutshell. I recommend trying to Nutshell every movie you see, including ones not in this book.

Pay particular attention to what is happening at right before 25% into the running time (0:30:00 in a 120-minute movie). This is when the POINT OF NO RETURN and its CATCH should occur. The other anchor to look for is around 75% into the running time (1:30:00 in a 120-minute movie). This is roughly when the protagonist will reach either their CRISIS (if it is an Aristotelian comedy) or their TRIUMPH (if it is a tragedy). For the Film Nutshells in Part 4 and cross-referenced in the text, I've indicated the exact time when these two anchors occur, as well as expressed them as a percentage of the total running time. As you read this book, I'll give you more tips on how to identify other Nutshell elements.

Then try using the Nutshell Technique for your own screenplays. The easiest, most straightforward way to use it is when you are beginning a story from scratch, before a word of the screenplay is written. The Nutshell Technique form has you isolate eight essential elements of the story and gives you a visual means to check that these important interconnections are working. It's much, much easier to confirm that they are working (and to fix them if they are not) when they exist only on a one-page schematic than to try to fix them after you've finished a 120-page screenplay.

You probably could write a paragraph or more on each of the eight elements, but you should try to fit your answers into the boxes provided. Nothing should be longer than a sentence. A phrase is often enough. You should force yourself to boil it down. You are being asked to isolate these eight story elements buried beneath all these plot details swirling around in your head. The Nutshell Technique is not designed to convey every nuance of your story. It's about getting to these eight key elements that make up the spine of your story, your story at its most essential. The Nutshell Technique form allows you to see all the elements on one page so you can verify that the interdependencies are working and that your story is structurally sound.

You'll want to jump around on the Nutshell Technique form. Many writers will initially have a sense of the POINT OF NO RETURN or their protagonist's FLAW. Start with what you think you know. A big part of the process is discovering what you're "married to." Does your CATCH test the protagonist's FLAW? If not, which element are you willing to change, the CATCH or the FLAW, in order to make the story work better?

For all films I discuss, the corresponding screenplays to which I refer—the final drafts—will be assumed to be consistent with what we see on screen, regardless of other drafts that may exist in print. The filmmakers made the final determination of what and when things occur, and so the film itself is our best source of the script. When I quote dialogue, it is taken verbatim from the actual film, not the screenplay. Exceptions are noted.

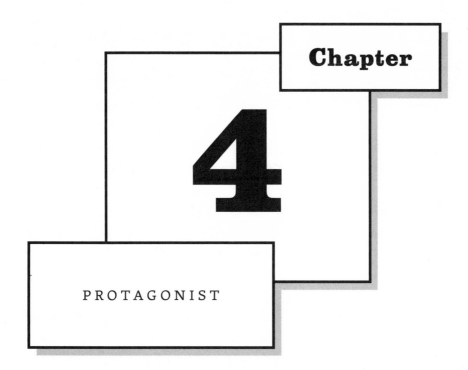

Chapter

4

PROTAGONIST

Film Nutshells Discussed in This Chapter

The Bourne Identity
Little Miss Sunshine
The Sixth Sense
Titanic
The Usual Suspects

TO USE THE NUTSHELL TECHNIQUE, you must identify one protagonist. Even in *Butch Cassidy and the Sundance Kid* (not Nutshelled) or *Harold and Kumar Go to White Castle* (not Nutshelled), only one of the titular characters is the protagonist—from the writer's point of view, anyway—whether the audience realizes it or not. One character is the protagonist because, while the audience may perceive it as a "buddy picture," on a subconscious level they can only fully and truly identify with one character over the course of an entire storyline. The audience may feel empathy at moments for characters other than the protagonist and may even change allegiances throughout the film. But in the end, just one character will fully align with the audience's own moral compass, or in the case of a tragedy, run counter to it.

So how do you determine who the protagonist is if it is not obvious? Most screenwriting theorists would define the protagonist as being the character who is pushing the action forward and making most of the tough choices. But to use the Nutshell Technique, the protagonist is going to be determined by looking at the characters' relationships to their central FLAWs.

In an Aristotelian comedy, the protagonist is the one who makes the most significant change in terms of their central FLAW, and they learn its opposite in the end—their STRENGTH—like Harold does when he finally finds the courage to stand up to his bullying co-worker and then to ask out his pretty neighbor (incidentally, the protagonist in the sequel is Kumar). In a tragedy, the protagonist is the one who fails to change from their FLAW more significantly and therefore fails to gain their potential STRENGTH in the end, like Butch when he proclaims, "For a moment there, I thought we were in trouble," right before he leads the two in bursting out blazing into their demise in an ambush of a hundred Bolivian soldiers.

Identifying the protagonist is going to be easier for some stories than for others. Yes, Rocky Balboa is the protagonist of *Rocky* (not Nutshelled), and Jason Bourne (Matt Damon) is the protagonist of *The Bourne Identity*. But in *Little Miss Sunshine*, the protagonist is not six-year-old Olive (Abigail Breslin), the little girl competing in the titular Little Miss Sunshine pageant.

Pre-teenage children aren't typically protagonists because, central to the protagonist—and, in fact, central to the entire story—is the protagonist's FLAW and the protagonist's ability to overcome it (comedy) or not (tragedy). Children don't have major FLAWs that need to be overcome. In the eyes of the audience, they're largely innocent. There's nothing wrong with Olive that needs to change; there's no big STRENGTH she needs to gain. She is just a little girl. But she's beginning to internalize society's unhealthy ideas about beauty and about what it means to be a "winner."

[34] What she needs are the adults around her, especially her father, Richard (Greg Kinnear), to wake up to what their unhealthy influence is exposing her to. The fact is that she isn't beauty pageant material, and the cruel

reality is that she is going to humiliate herself if her father doesn't intervene. Richard is the protagonist because he has the greatest FLAW to overcome: he's <u>shallow</u>. His superficial view of a world that is simply made up of "winners" and "losers" has begun to infect his daughter, and he will be largely responsible for the pain she will endure if she finds out that most people would categorize her in the latter group. Richard, not Olive, is the one who needs to change and learn that his ridiculous idea of a world of only winners and losers is poisonous and only hurts him and those around him.

Since I've tipped you off that children aren't usually protagonists, you probably won't make the mistake, as some of my workshop writers do, of thinking that nine-year-old Cole is the protagonist in *The Sixth Sense*. It's an understandable mistake. Cole is the one with the titular "sixth sense": that is, the ability to see ghosts. And until the big reveal at the end of the film, it appears that Cole is the one with the problems that are at the heart of the story. He has been assigned (or so it appears) to child psychologist Dr. Malcolm Crowe (Bruce Willis) because he is terrified and troubled by these supposed encounters with ghostly visions.

But as you have probably guessed, Malcolm is the actual protagonist of *The Sixth Sense*. In a comedy, the protagonist will be the character who goes through the biggest change, whose FLAW is completely overcome to the point that they change as a person 180 degrees and gain as a STRENGTH whatever is the exact opposite of their FLAW. Yes, *The Sixth Sense* is an Aristotelian comedy. While it's a little sad to learn in the end that Malcolm was actually killed in the shooting at the beginning, we realize that Malcolm is much better off now. Had he not met Cole, Malcolm would have continued as a ghost roaming the earth, haunting his young widowed wife, not realizing he was dead, and continuing to obsess about having once let down a patient and about why he and his wife can't seem to communicate anymore. That would be a tragedy. But because he met Cole and helped Cole conquer his demons, Malcolm's story is a comedy. Malcolm was able to overcome his FLAW that he <u>lacks faith in himself</u> and gain the STRENGTH of <u>faith in himself</u>. He did everything that he could for his patients and he never put his wife second to his career. Now Malcolm can see all this and also see the truth for the first time: that he's a ghost. He can finally leave

[35]

his wife in peace, knowing that he did the best he could while on earth, and she will stop being haunted by him and will be able to move past her grief and on with her life.

Cole learns and changes, too. He learns from Malcolm not to be afraid of ghosts. In the end he coexists with the spirits around him without any distress and seems much happier and well adjusted. But it is Malcolm who has the most profound change; in a comedy, the protagonist will be the one who has the most profound change (or the most profoundly tragic failure to change, in a tragedy).

In the Aristotelian comedy *Titanic*, the protagonist is Rose (Kate Winslet). Yes, it's a comedy! Even though Jack (Leonardo DiCaprio) dies, in the end Rose gains the STRENGTH of bravery, and she completely changes the trajectory of the rest of her life. Jack's story seems like a tragic story, but he's not the protagonist. His FLAW didn't bring him down. The Aristotelian concept of tragedy is about having an opportunity to change and to face something in yourself, something in your control. Jack's story is not about that. The ship's sinking is out of his control.

Of course the ship sinking is out of her control, too, but the sinking and Jack's death bring to light for Rose certain things that *are* in her control. From this experience, she gains the STRENGTH to take charge of her own destiny; if she can survive this ordeal, she can change the course of her life completely. Jack is really something of a dramatic pawn in the story. Dramatically he exists in the story to bring Rose through this transformation, to help Rose gain the STRENGTH of bravery.

By the way, probably 95% of movies out there, for better or worse, are Aristotelian comedies. Hollywood couldn't even do the story of the *Titanic* without making it an Aristotelian comedy! A big generalization is that audiences don't want to see a "downer." But this doesn't mean that a film that is structurally a tragedy can't be a success. Fewer of them are made, but also fewer are written.

Let's look at *The Usual Suspects*. It's referred to as an ensemble film, meaning a film that, instead of having a sole protagonist, has multiple significant characters, each of whom is assigned a roughly equal amount of importance and screen time. While the general viewing audience may perceive it as an ensemble film, in fact *The Usual Suspects* does have a sole protagonist. Who is it?

[36]

Who's the protagonist? (Hint: none of the above.) Still from *The Usual Suspects*. Copyright 1995, Rosco Film GmbH and Bad Hat Harry Productions, Inc.

When I ask this question in my workshops, most writers say Verbal Kint (Kevin Spacey). He is the one telling the story-within-a-story. He's also an important character in both that story-within-a-story as well as in the present action of the officials trying to get to the bottom of what happened in the ship explosion.

In the end, the customs agent realizes Verbal made the whole story up, but Verbal has already slipped away in a waiting getaway car. Verbal has a happy ending, which suggests that if he were the protagonist, the story would be an Aristotelian comedy. But in an Aristotelian comedy, the protagonist has a happy ending due at least in part to their ability to change from a central FLAW to its opposite, the STRENGTH. Verbal undergoes no such change. He cleverly and confidently outwits the officials and disappears, unscathed and unchanged. Therefore he is not the protagonist.

The next character my writers will pick as their candidate for protagonist is Dean Keaton (Gabriel Byrne). His story may be the most intriguing. A formerly corrupt police officer trying to go straight, he is pulled back into the criminal world when he joins Verbal and three others in committing a few heists. He may or may not have double-crossed his partners and is possibly Keyser Soze, who, according to Verbal, is a legendary, almost mythic figure of the underworld.

The problem with Dean Keaton as protagonist is that the movie viewer knows very little about what really happened to him. His tale is related by Verbal, who we discover in the end made up most everything we heard. The customs agent questioning Verbal, David Kujan (Chazz Palminteri), has been doing so because he's after Dean Keaton, so Dean Keaton does exist in the world of this story. But anything relayed by Verbal—the whole story-within-the-story—is likely the product of his gifted imagination. As a result, we have no idea what the fate of Dean Keaton was, and so it is impossible to know whether he changed from a FLAW or not. He cannot be the protagonist.

It is Agent Kujan, you may have now surmised, who is the protagonist. He realizes too late that Verbal made the whole story up and that he has let this criminal mastermind go free. His ending is a sad one, making him a tragic protagonist. In a tragedy, the protagonist fails to change from their FLAW to the STRENGTH. His FLAW, that he's arrogant, makes him blind to the fact that not only is Verbal making the whole thing up, he's using objects from the very room they are in to spin his tall tale.

Specifying only one protagonist will make things easier, especially if you are writing a buddy picture or an ensemble picture. You can have multiple characters who are important, but only one has to meet all the required interdependencies on the Nutshell Technique form for your story to work. The reader doesn't have to know that this one character is the protagonist. They can perceive it as an ensemble story. Designating a sole protagonist is for the screenwriter's benefit, not the reader's or viewer's.

Chapter 5

SET-UP WANT: PART 1

The **SET-UP WANT**:

- is one of the things the protagonist wants in their first scene
- must be achieved by the protagonist in the POINT OF NO RETURN, but they will also get something they don't want, the CATCH
- must be the exact opposite of the CRISIS, in a comedy, or see its ideal manifestation in the TRIUMPH, in a tragedy

Film Nutshells Discussed in This Chapter

Argo
Sunset Blvd.
Groundhog Day

THE SET-UP WANT IS one of the things the protagonist wants. *One.* Not *all.* Not necessarily the thing they want the *most.* Not necessarily even the want that drives the character's motivations. It's just one thing, sometimes a little thing, that the protagonist wants.

We're going to find the SET-UP WANT in the protagonist's very first scene. Sometimes the WANT is verbalized by the protagonist, and sometimes it's not. Your protagonist must get their SET-UP WANT in the POINT OF NO RETURN, but they will get the WANT along with something they *don't* want, and the thing that they don't want is the CATCH.

In *Argo*, what is protagonist Tony Mendez's SET-UP WANT?

It's 1979, and six Americans have escaped the US Embassy in Iran right before the Iranian takeover. They are now hiding out in the Canadian Embassy, but it is a matter of time before the Iranians will realize six Americans are missing and find and execute them. The State Department wants to rescue them, and they call in Tony Mendez (Ben Affleck), the CIA's "best exfil guy" (exfiltration, or extraction, specialist), to hear their ideas. But Tony points to major problems in each of their plans. None of them is tenable.

Tony's SET-UP WANT is <u>a plan to get the six Americans out of Iran</u>.

He gets his WANT in the POINT OF NO RETURN: <u>*Planet of the Apes* is on TV, and he gets an escape plan</u>. They'll say they're in Iran scouting locations for a sci-fi movie. But there's a CATCH: <u>it requires they look like a real film overnight</u>.

In *Sunset Blvd.*, what is protagonist Joe Gillis's SET-UP WANT?

In his bathrobe, Joe (William Holden) is typing away. His voiceover informs us that he's a screenwriter with a couple of B pictures to his credit. He hasn't worked for a studio for a long time. He's been cranking out screenplay pitches, but no one has been buying. His door buzzer rings, and it's two repo guys here for his car. His voiceover tells us that he needs money fast or he'll lose his car.

Joe's SET-UP WANT is <u>a writing job</u>.

He gets his SET-UP WANT in the POINT OF NO RETURN: his car breaks down at the mansion of a former silent film star, and she <u>hires him to rewrite a script for her comeback</u>. The CATCH is <u>the script is terrible, and she is delusional</u>.

[40]   In both of these examples, the protagonist's SET-UP WANT and how the protagonist gets their WANT in the POINT OF NO RETURN is relatively straightforward. But more often, the connection between the two isn't so obvious. In fact, often in a film it will appear that the protagonist *didn't* get what they wanted in the POINT OF NO RETURN.

For example in *Groundhog Day*, Phil is a local TV weatherman in Pittsburgh, and in his first scene, he says that a major network is interested in him. Clearly he wants to be a big network weatherman. The POINT OF NO RETURN is when he wakes up, and it's Groundhog Day again; the day won't move forward. In the POINT OF NO RETURN does Phil get his want to be a big network weatherman? No, he doesn't. It's something he wants—something big and ambitious, even—but in terms of story structure, it's not his SET-UP WANT.

Just as real people want many things in life, fictional characters also want many things. The key to the SET-UP WANT/POINT OF NO RETURN relationship is to find *one* WANT that the protagonist actually gets in the POINT OF NO RETURN. There is something that Phil the weatherman gets in the POINT OF NO RETURN, when the day won't move forward, that he actually wants. What is it?

The SET-UP WANT is the first of the eight Nutshell elements on the Nutshell Technique form because it's revealed somewhere in the protagonist's very first scene, making it the first of the elements to appear over the course of the film's running time or on the page in a screenplay. The protagonist has multiple wants, but there is only one POINT OF NO RETURN, which means finding a SET-UP WANT/POINT OF NO RETURN match can be difficult. Making it even harder is the fact that the SET-UP WANT must, in a comedy, be the opposite of the CRISIS (in a tragedy, the TRIUMPH is the ultimate manifestation of the SET-UP WANT).

For these reasons, it is important to explain the POINT OF NO RETURN first, which is what I'll do in the next chapter, and then I'll come back to discuss the SET-UP WANT further in Chapter 7, where I'll also reveal what Phil the weatherman's SET-UP WANT is.

When writers are applying the Nutshell Technique to their own stories in my workshops, I tell them to skip the SET-UP WANT and go straight to identifying the POINT OF NO RETURN first, which I recommend you do, too.

[41]

The **POINT OF NO RETURN**:

- brings the protagonist their first-scene SET-UP WANT
- brings the protagonist an immediate CATCH, which is what the protagonist got in the POINT OF NO RETURN that they *didn't* want

Also:

- it's a turning point that makes this story *this story*
- it signals the end of Act 1 and the beginning of Act 2
- it happens by the 25% point in the screenplay/film, which means it almost always happens between page 20 and page 30 (ideally close to page 25) or between 0:20:00 and 0:30:00 into the running time
- it happens *to* the protagonist

Film Nutshells Discussed in This Chapter

The Bourne Identity
Witness

The Usual Suspects
Titanic
The Sixth Sense
Casablanca
Groundhog Day

BY THE END OF THE first quarter of the film, something will have happened to the protagonist that completely changes the course of events in their life. Most every screenwriting theorist agrees that you really need this strong event around 25 pages into the screenplay, or 25 minutes into the film's running time, to push the protagonist into Act 2. Screenwriters refer to this element using various terms, such as Plot Point 1, the Break into Act 2, the Big Event, the First Reversal, or the Act 1 Climax. (It's also sometimes incorrectly referred to as the Inciting Incident; see text box below.) The term I use is the POINT OF NO RETURN.

The **Inciting Incident** is an event that precedes the POINT OF NO RETURN, occurring around 0:05:00–0:10:00 in the film or pages 5–10 in the screenplay. It is, as the name suggests, an incident that incites the protagonist, and it will move them toward the POINT OF NO RETURN. The Inciting Incident often has to occur in order for the POINT OF NO RETURN to be a point of no return. The Inciting Incident is not part of the Nutshell Technique because it has no interdependencies with the Nutshell elements. It does precipitate the POINT OF NO RETURN, but one Inciting Incident can be changed into a completely different Inciting Incident without affecting the story's Nutshell. Some screenwriting theorists put undue emphasis on the Inciting Incident. I find that in having to delay the POINT OF NO RETURN to page 25, writers tend to naturally create an Inciting Incident along the way. I mention it only because it is another important event in Act 1, and it is often mistaken for the POINT OF NO RETURN.

It's often said that the story *really* begins with Act 2. You can't get a better delineated example of the break from Act 1 into Act 2 than in *The Wizard of Oz* (not Nutshelled) when the film switches from black and white to color. "Toto, I've a feeling we're not in Kansas anymore!" Dorothy exclaims. The POINT OF NO RETURN for Dorothy is: a tornado uproots her house and drops it in the Land of Oz. In your story, you want to shoot for a POINT OF NO RETURN that gives us that same feeling as we enter your second act: everything has changed for the protagonist forever; the world has gone from black and white to color; and we're no longer in Kansas, Toto. Often, but not always, there is a literal change of location when we enter Act 2. It's a great metaphor to use because the protagonist is always entering a figurative New World in Act 2.

The POINT OF NO RETURN is an event that changes everything for the protagonist. But watch out—there are lots of events in a movie. Almost every scene in your script is going to be an event of some sort. In a film, if we see a scene that just shows the banal landscape of suburbia, perhaps to mirror the banal inner life the protagonist is experiencing, it probably wasn't in the screenplay. It's likely something the film's director added. Because in a screenplay, every scene is to an extent an event. Some events are just more important than others. And there is one event that is bigger than all the rest.

And even describing the POINT OF NO RETURN as an event that changes everything is a little misleading, because there are a couple of events in every screenplay that change everything. But this event is the one that *really* changes everything. This is the event that pushes the protagonist past a point of no return where there is no going back to the way things used to be. This POINT OF NO RETURN makes the film *the* film that it is, and due to its vital function, the POINT OF NO RETURN is often reflected in the film's title.

In *The Bourne Identity*, what is protagonist Jason Bourne's SET-UP WANT?

In the first scenes of the film, some Italian fishermen spy Bourne floating unconscious in the ocean and drag him aboard their boat. One fisherman pulls out a medical kit and surgically removes two bullets from Bourne's back. Suddenly Bourne regains consciousness and attacks the fisherman, demanding to know what the man is doing to him and where he is. The fisherman explains that they pulled him out of the water and calms him down, saying, "I'm your friend. My name is Giancarlo. Who are you? What's your name?" Bourne has amnesia and says, "I don't know," and then he passes out. Bourne's SET-UP WANT is to figure out who he is.

Now what's the POINT OF NO RETURN for him, the moment that's going to put him on the journey that makes this film the film we know as *The Bourne Identity*?

When I ask this question in my screenwriting workshops, writers sometimes cite the scene in which two Zurich police officers wake a sleeping Bourne in the park. He instantly springs into action, and in seven seconds, Bourne has one of their guns and both men on the ground, completely incapacitated. It's an important moment, because it's the first time we, the audience, see he has incredible combat skills, and he's surprised by it, too. He looks alarmed to be holding a gun, and he disengages it, drops it, and runs. But it doesn't put us past a POINT OF NO RETURN on the journey that will become the film *The Bourne Identity*.

At 0:10:39–0:11:34, this scene is too early to be the POINT OF NO RETURN. More important, this isn't a moment that changes everything. Bourne has learned a little about himself—he's apparently had some kind of defense training—but he's not past a POINT OF NO RETURN that makes this story *this* story. When this scene with the police happens, Bourne could have done a lot of different things. He could have turned himself in or fled the country. There were a number of reactions he could have had at this moment that would have taken us on a completely different story path, and theoretically led to the creation of a different screenplay than the one we know as *The Bourne Identity*. So this altercation in itself doesn't change everything; it doesn't put us past the POINT OF NO RETURN we should feel when we leave Act 1 and everything goes, figuratively speaking, from black and white to color.

To do this takes opening the Swiss bank safe-deposit box and discovering what's inside—a passport that says he's Jason Bourne, plus additional passports with other identities for him, a gun, and a lot of cash, which all together look ominous. Had he not opened the safe-deposit box because, say, he never got the account numbers, or if the Zurich police officers had put him in jail, or if he opened the safe-deposit box but it contained only some old watches, he wouldn't have found out he's a man with multiple identities and an ominous past, and the story wouldn't be *The Bourne Iden-*

[46]

tity. It would have been a different film altogether. While the police scene adds a little to our understanding of the protagonist, technically we could have cut it out of the script. The script might not have been as good, but it would still work. If, however, we cut out the safe-deposit box scene, the movie wouldn't work or even make any sense, since Bourne finding out he's a man with multiple identities and an ominous past drives the rest of the story.

Notice that Bourne gets his first-scene SET-UP WANT: to figure out who he is. In the POINT OF NO RETURN, when he opens the safe-deposit box, he finds out who he is. We're going to find this in *every* screenplay that succeeds in telling a structurally sound story. This is a critical concept that I'm going to come back to a few times: we're going to find *something* that the protagonist wants in their first scene that they are going to get in the POINT OF NO RETURN. They won't get *everything* they want. They might not get the thing they want the most. They may not even get the thing they said they wanted. But in the POINT OF NO RETURN, they are going to get *something* that they wanted in their first scene.

Note also that the POINT OF NO RETURN is something that happens *to* the protagonist. The other seven elements of the Nutshell are largely internal to the protagonist: their WANT, their FLAW, their CLIMACTIC CHOICE, and so on. But the POINT OF NO RETURN is the one thing on the Nutshell Technique form that has to happen *to* the protagonist for this story to be set in motion. If it hadn't happened to him—if Bourne never opened the safe-deposit box and never found out about his multiple identities—we'd be watching a completely different story. I don't know what film it would be, but it wouldn't be called *The Bourne Identity.*

To be clear about the fact that the POINT OF NO RETURN happens *to* the protagonist, I encourage writers to find a way to express it so that the protagonist isn't the subject of the sentence when you fill in your POINT OF NO RETURN description. This will be a rare instance when you should use the passive voice. So, don't write the POINT OF NO RETURN like this: "Bourne opens a safe-deposit box which reveals that he is Jason Bourne and has multiple passports, a gun, and cash." A better way to write it, for [47] our purposes, is this: a safe-deposit box reveals he's Jason Bourne and has multiple passports, a gun, and cash (14–15%: 0:15:57–0:18:21). It can sound a little convoluted sometimes, but it's a good way to check that your POINT

OF NO RETURN is something external happening *to* the protagonist and not something they simply choose to do one day. We need an external POINT OF NO RETURN to happen and change the course of events in our protagonist's life one day. Had this POINT OF NO RETURN not occurred, this story wouldn't have occurred.

The POINT OF NO RETURN and the CATCH are immediately and directly connected. I'll discuss the CATCH in more detail in the chapter devoted to it, but for now, I want to make you aware of the CATCH's relationship to the POINT OF NO RETURN, because you'll need to keep the CATCH in mind when you are determining the POINT OF NO RETURN. With the POINT OF NO RETURN, the protagonist is going to get their SET-UP WANT, but they are also going to get something they didn't want, and that is the CATCH.

Here is the WANT/POINT OF NO RETURN/CATCH progression for Jason Bourne:

SET-UP WANT:	to figure out who he is
POINT OF NO RETURN:	a safe-deposit box reveals he's Jason Bourne and has multiple passports, a gun, and cash
CATCH:	looks like he's a dangerous criminal

The CATCH is usually a part of the POINT OF NO RETURN itself and does not require any additional scenes. Jason doesn't find out later that he might be a criminal. The moment he looks in that safe-deposit box he knows, and so does the audience. In getting his SET-UP WANT (to figure out who he is), he simultaneously gets something he didn't want, the CATCH (looks like he's a dangerous criminal).

The CATCH is not a problem that emerges later in Act 2 or something that the protagonist discovers in Act 2 or 3, although often there are other developments that happen late in Act 2 that one might call "catches." These late "catches," however, are not the Nutshell CATCH. The Nutshell CATCH happens as a part of the POINT OF NO RETURN and therefore before the break into Act 2.

[48]

If the CATCH is not completely simultaneous with the protagonist getting the WANT in the POINT OF NO RETURN, it is at the very least an immediate result of the POINT OF NO RETURN. Because the POINT OF

NO RETURN must give the protagonist their WANT and also bring them a CATCH, sometimes what comprises the full POINT OF NO RETURN may stretch over a couple of scenes and even be made up of two or three connected events.

In *Witness,* for example, protagonist Detective John Book's (Harrison Ford) first-scene SET-UP WANT is to find the killer. He gets his WANT when his witness to the murder, an Amish boy, happens to see a picture of the police officer who was the killer. It seems like we have the CATCH—the killer is a cop in his own department—but there's a much bigger CATCH to reveal itself very shortly. In the next scene, Book goes to tell his mentor, the deputy chief on the force, who tells Book to keep this between the two of them. Then the next scene: after parking in his apartment building garage, Book turns to find the killer cop, who shoots at him, and they engage in gunfire until the killer cop flees.

Now we have a real CATCH: not only is a cop in his department a killer, his beloved mentor is in on the conspiracy (because how else would the killer cop have known Book knew he was the killer and therefore tried to kill him?). In order to ensure that the POINT OF NO RETURN description reveals that Book got his SET-UP WANT along with what he didn't want (the CATCH), this is how I worded the POINT OF NO RETURN: the boy identifies a cop as the killer, Book tells his mentor, and the killer cop tries to kill Book (25–29%: 0:27:50–0:32:13).

In this POINT OF NO RETURN, Book gets his SET-UP WANT (to find the killer) along with a huge CATCH: his mentor is in on the conspiracy. Book isn't dealing with just one rogue cop. He's dealing with a cover-up that reaches at least as far up as his deputy chief and has stakes high enough to move his mentor (a friend with whom Book is so close as to be on a first-name basis with the deputy's entire family) to try to have Book killed.

When you use the Nutshell Technique form to develop your own story, make sure you write out your description of the POINT OF NO RETURN so that it includes everything that happens from when the protagonist gets their SET-UP WANT through when the CATCH reveals itself to them either simultaneously with or immediately after the POINT OF NO RETURN. The POINT OF NO RETURN must occur and the CATCH must be apparent to the protagonist before the end of Act 1, which would be by roughly page 30 in a 120-page script (25% into the script).

[49]

The CATCH is not a new event. It does not require scenes in addition to the POINT OF NO RETURN, although as we saw in the example of *Witness*, it may require the POINT OF NO RETURN to encompass more than one scene. Think of the CATCH as me asking you to spell out your answer to my question: in the POINT OF NO RETURN your protagonist got their SET-UP WANT, but what did they get that they *didn't* want? What they get that they didn't want is the CATCH, and there has to be an up-front CATCH. If you don't have a CATCH, then you've just given your protagonist exactly their WANT, and there's no longer any conflict. And once there is no more conflict, your story is essentially over.

Again, the Nutshell CATCH is not something the protagonist discovers later, in Act 2 or 3. It is an immediate problem that comes as a part of the POINT OF NO RETURN. Also, the CATCH is always from the protagonist's point of view. Your protagonist must recognize at the time of the POINT OF NO RETURN that, in addition to getting their WANT, they also got something they *didn't* want.

In *The Usual Suspects*, for example, the protagonist is US customs agent Dave Kujan, and the POINT OF NO RETURN for him is the police sergeant lets him talk to Verbal (21%: 0:21:53–0:22:22). But the CATCH is *not* "the whole thing is a story Verbal made up," nor is it "Verbal is Keyser Soze," although these are big "catches" that will reveal themselves at the very end of the film. The Nutshell CATCH must be from the protagonist's point of view at the time of the POINT OF NO RETURN, and at the time of the POINT OF NO RETURN, Kujan has no clue that what he is about to hear is a complete fabrication. The CATCH from Kujan's point of view at the time of the POINT OF NO RETURN is Verbal is a physically challenged simpleton with total immunity.

I don't like to make rules, but your POINT OF NO RETURN and its CATCH really need to happen before page 30, and they shouldn't happen before page 20. Sometimes I see the POINT OF NO RETURN happen on the screen as early as 0:15:00, but I wouldn't advise writing one at page 15. In those cases, if you look at the original screenplays, you usually will find that the POINT OF NO RETURN didn't occur on the page until closer to page 25, but sometimes on the screen it creeps up.

It's not a bad thing at all to have the POINT OF NO RETURN work like clockwork and fall right on page 25. Ignore this at your own peril! When you watch films, try to keep an accurate eye on the running time and check what is happening on the screen at exactly 25 minutes into the film. You'll be surprised how often the POINT OF NO RETURN happens at 25 minutes on the nose.

The POINT OF NO RETURN and its CATCH signal the break from Act 1 into Act 2 at around 25% of the way into the film, so this "25 page/25 minute" guideline is roughly proportional to the film's total running time. If a movie has a 100-minute total running time, 25% of 100 is 25. So the POINT OF NO RETURN should begin and end by 0:25:00 into the film, meaning the POINT OF NO RETURN might begin around 0:22:00, but it should occur and the impact of its CATCH be apparent all by 0:25:00. If a movie is on the short side, say with a total running time of 90 minutes, 25% of 90 is 22.5. So in this case the POINT OF NO RETURN probably would occur closer to 0:22:30.

This proportionality guideline also applies to longer films. In *Titanic*, the POINT OF NO RETURN doesn't happen until 0:38:16–0:43:56, but let me remind you that (1) the film has a 194-minute running time, and 25% of 194 is 0:48:00, so the POINT OF NO RETURN is still occurring before the 25% point, and (2) you are not James Cameron! A 194-minute running time translates to an estimated 194-page script! Without having clout in the film industry, you will find it universally advised to keep your script at 120 pages maximum. Readers are very unhappy to flip to the last page and find a higher number of pages. And in a script of up to 120 pages, you are well advised to have your POINT OF NO RETURN occur by page 30 at the latest.

So unless you are James Cameron, your POINT OF NO RETURN really can't go over page 30 even by a few pages. If it does, your reader is very likely to put your script down at page 30 and not pick it back up. There's just something in our psychology, in how we've internalized the principles of storytelling, that lead us to expect something big by that point. If it hasn't happened by then, we feel like the plot is too meandering and going nowhere, and we lose interest. Thirty minutes/30 pages seems to be the tipping point by which we must enter Act 2, which is one of the purposes of the POINT OF NO RETURN: it signals the clear demarcation that we are leaving Act 1, when the world was black and white, and entering the new and colorful land that is Act 2.

Note also the POINT OF NO RETURN in *Titanic* is *not* hitting the iceberg, which happens at 1:39:31 (not so incidentally, the iceberg is first spotted at 1:37:12, exactly at the midpoint of the film's 194-minute total running time). The POINT OF NO RETURN occurs after Jack convinces Rose not to jump: she falls overboard, but Jack saves her (20–23%: 0:38:16–0:43:56). Had Jack not happened upon her as she was about to jump, she would have jumped, assuming that she herself or someone other than Jack didn't talk her out of it. In either case, she wouldn't have met Jack, their romance wouldn't have begun, and she would have just been another *Titanic* survivor (or casualty). She wouldn't have had this special story to tell. But because she meets Jack, this POINT OF NO RETURN is the beginning of her transformation into a better person. *That's* the real story. We already know the ship is going to sink, but we don't know what will happen to Rose once she meets Jack.

The POINT OF NO RETURN should be stated on the Nutshell Technique form from the protagonist's point of view. For example, in *The Sixth Sense*, the POINT OF NO RETURN is not "Malcolm is killed" or "Malcolm's actually a ghost." In the film, Dr. Malcolm Crowe is shot by Vincent, a former patient, at 0:10:12. At the very end of the film he (and we) first discover that Malcolm was actually killed back when that happened, and everything we saw after the shooting was based on his misperception (and ours) that he survived the shooting. But of course we ultimately learn he didn't.

So Malcolm getting shot is not the POINT OF NO RETURN. First of all, 0:10:12 is too early for the POINT OF NO RETURN. Second, the protagonist must get their SET-UP WANT in the POINT OF NO RETURN, and I can't think of anything Malcolm wanted that he got in getting shot. And third, from Malcolm's point of view, he thinks he is still alive until the end of the movie. The POINT OF NO RETURN must be about what changes everything according to the *protagonist* at that point in the movie. Being killed in the shooting and becoming a ghost can't be the POINT OF NO RETURN because Malcolm doesn't realize that this has happened.

Now, he does think the shooting changed things in his marriage, marking the point at which he and his wife began having trouble communicating. The shooting was an important event (in fact the shooting was the Inciting Incident). But there are many important events in a movie. The shooting in itself does not put us on the course that will make this film *The Sixth Sense* and not some other film. We're not out of Kansas yet, Toto.

Remember: the POINT OF NO RETURN is often reflected in the title. What makes *The Sixth Sense* "The Sixth Sense"? Well, "the sixth sense" refers to the ability to see ghosts, and we're introduced to this concept when young Cole famously tells Malcolm, "I see dead people." When does this happen? Not until 0:50:26, way, way too late to qualify as the POINT OF NO RETURN.

Okay, so let's look at what's happening at the end of Act 1, in particular at that sweet spot right around 25 minutes into the running time. At 0:21:35, Malcolm meets with Cole in their supposed first therapy session at Cole's house. Cole reveals he drew a violent picture at school, and he tells Malcolm as their session ends at 0:26:06: "You're nice, but you can't help me." Then Malcolm arrives late to his anniversary dinner (or so it appears), where he proclaims to his wife that with Cole he's being given a second chance. Cole becomes his second chance (21–24%: 0:21:35–0:26:06) is the POINT OF NO RETURN.

To the audience, it may not seem significant, but for Malcolm, it's a very important development. As he explains to his wife (or thinks he does), Cole is just like Vincent, the former patient who shot him, when Vincent was a child. Remember, the POINT OF NO RETURN both (1) changes the course of events for the protagonist and (2) gives the protagonist something they wanted in their first dialogue scene.

So what is Malcolm's first-scene SET-UP WANT?

In his first scene, he and his wife are tipsily celebrating after he received an award from the mayor for professional excellence as a child psychologist. She praises her husband's "gift," which is to teach "children how to be strong in situations where most adults would piss on themselves." Malcolm's SET-UP WANT is to help kids in the most difficult situations. It's his life's work. Even when he is confronted in the second scene by a clearly disturbed Vincent, who has broken into his home and accuses the psychologist of failing him, Malcolm tells Vincent he can try to help him now.

Does Malcolm get his WANT, to help kids in difficult situations, in the POINT OF NO RETURN when Cole becomes his second chance? Yes, he

[53]

wants to help kids in difficult situations, and while he failed Vincent, now with Cole he's getting a second chance to help a troubled kid with a similar psychological profile. He thinks helping Cole will redeem him for the guilt he feels for having failed Vincent.

Generally we should feel a big shift with the POINT OF NO RETURN, because this is the moment we are wrapping up the black-and-white world of Act 1 and are entering the colorful land of Oz that is Act 2. The first time you saw *The Sixth Sense*, assuming no one spoiled it for you, you probably felt the shift with the POINT OF NO RETURN when Cole becomes his second chance. It was only after you finished the movie and realized Malcolm was a ghost this whole time that your perception changed, and you may have felt Malcolm getting shot by Vincent was the POINT OF NO RETURN. But the POINT OF NO RETURN is from the *protagonist's* point of view. From Malcolm's point of view, Cole becoming his patient is the POINT OF NO RETURN, and the moment that Cole becomes his second chance drives the rest of his story.

If Cole had not come into his life and become his patient, the story and film we know as *The Sixth Sense* never would have happened. In the original script[1] Malcolm says explicitly that he hasn't been able to work since the shooting, although this bit of dialogue didn't make it into the film. His failure to help Vincent, he believes, has made him afraid of failing other children. But upon meeting Cole, Malcolm sees that he has a real opportunity to help a kid no one else can help, and if he can accomplish this, it will give him back the confidence he needs in order to return to practicing child psychology for the most difficult cases. Since the shooting, Malcolm feels that he and his wife have grown apart (which, of course, they have, but for a reason different from what Malcolm thinks), and he hopes that this second chance to help a troubled kid will also give him a second chance with his marriage by giving him an opportunity to learn how to balance work and married life.

[54]   Notice that it's no accident that *this* psychologist (a doctor who has lost confidence in his abilities) got *this* patient (a kid whom no one else has been able to help). Nor is it an accident that *this* patient (a kid haunted by troubled ghosts) got *this* psychologist (a troubled ghost who is also a gifted child psychologist). Putting these two together was not a random decision. This is not merely a situation. This, truly, is a story.

It's no accident the screenwriter brought these two characters together. Still from *The Sixth Sense*. Copyright 1999, Spyglass Entertainment Group, LP.

The POINT OF NO RETURN is often reflected in the title, although some-times we don't find out exactly how until closer to the middle of the movie. Sometimes the title relates to the POINT OF NO RETURN and the protago-nist in more ways than one, and when that happens, it's a good thing, be-cause irony is a powerful tool for the writer.

For example, in *The Bourne Identity*, the POINT OF NO RETURN is <u>a safe-deposit box reveals he's Jason Bourne and has multiple passports, a gun, and cash</u>. It is in precisely this moment that Bourne finds out the first piece about his identity: he is someone with many identities and an ominous past. At the same time, it is just the beginning of his journey to get to the bottom of who he really is, an identity, he will eventually discover, with which he wants nothing to do.

In *The Sixth Sense*, the film's title also relates to the POINT OF NO RE-TURN and the protagonist in more ways than one. At the time of the POINT OF NO RETURN, <u>Cole becomes his second chance</u>, the implication is that Malcolm is the one with a sixth sense. His sixth sense is his ability to help the kids no one else can. At 0:50:26, Cole winds up in the hospital, where he first reveals to Malcolm, "I see dead people." Now we realize that Cole is the one with the titular sixth sense, the ability to see ghosts. [55]

The Sixth Sense is also a good example of something we often (but don't always) see in the POINT OF NO RETURN: it is giving the protagonist a second chance to face something they previously failed. Similarly in *Casablanca*, protagonist Rick (Humphrey Bogart) is getting a second chance with the woman who broke his heart, Ilsa, when in the POINT OF NO RETURN suddenly Ilsa walks into his bar on the arm of a war hero (24–32%: 0:25:18–0:33:35). As Rick laments, "Of all the gin joints in all the towns in all the world, she walks into mine!"

Groundhog Day takes giving the protagonist a second chance to an extreme: the POINT OF NO RETURN is the day won't move forward, and the universe is making Phil the weatherman repeat the same day over and over until he finally gets it right.

Having your protagonist face something they have previously failed in the POINT OF NO RETURN can be an excellent test of character. It's by no means a requirement for the POINT OF NO RETURN, but it's almost always a good thing to have.

The POINT OF NO RETURN is the crucial event that makes your story *this* story. It brings your protagonist their SET-UP WANT along with something they don't want (the CATCH). It should give us the sense that they have forever left behind the sepia-toned realm of yesterday as they now enter the Brand New World of Act 2, seen in all its Technicolor glory.

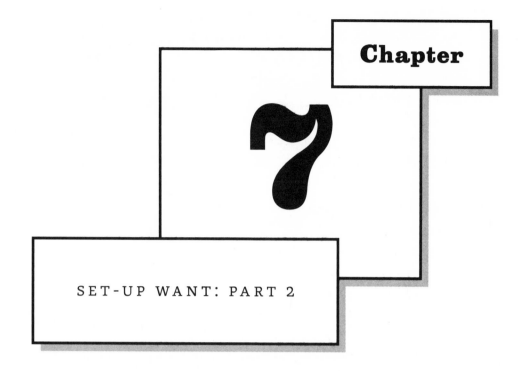

Chapter

7

SET-UP WANT: PART 2

The **SET-UP WANT:**

- is one of the things the protagonist wants in their first scene
- must be achieved by the protagonist in the POINT OF NO RETURN, but they will also get something they don't want, the CATCH
- must be the exact opposite of the CRISIS, in a comedy, or see its ideal manifestation in the TRIUMPH, in a tragedy

Film Nutshells Discussed in This Chapter

The Bourne Identity
Groundhog Day
Collateral
Juno

THE SET-UP WANT MAY BE the most difficult element of the Nutshell Technique to understand, which is why I'm devoting another chapter to it with one straightforward example and a few not-so-straightforward examples.

In the protagonist's very first scene, their SET-UP WANT should be established explicitly, although the protagonist may or may not verbalize it directly. The SET-UP WANT is just that: a set-up. We're setting up the old maxim "be careful what you wish for." Your protagonist wished for the SET-UP WANT to happen to them. On some level, they asked for it. And in the POINT OF NO RETURN they get it—along with a CATCH.

The Bourne Identity is a very clear example to illustrate the SET-UP WANT/POINT OF NO RETURN/CATCH relationship because the progression is obvious. In his first dialogue scene, Bourne clearly wants to figure out who he is, and he gets this WANT in the POINT OF NO RETURN: a safe-deposit box reveals he's Jason Bourne and has multiple passports, a gun, and cash (14–15%: 0:15:57–0:18:21). So he finds out who he is in this POINT OF NO RETURN but there is a CATCH: it looks like he's a dangerous criminal. The relationship between the WANT, the POINT OF NO RETURN, and the CATCH is unambiguous. In most films, however, the SET-UP WANT/POINT OF NO RETURN/CATCH relationship is not so clear-cut.

The SET-UP WANT is the trickiest part of the Nutshell Technique because (1) the protagonist must get this SET-UP WANT in the POINT OF NO RETURN, and at the same time (2) the SET-UP WANT must, in a comedy, be the opposite of the CRISIS (in a tragedy, the SET-UP WANT sees its ultimate manifestation in the TRIUMPH). It must meet both criteria, and this ain't easy. Sometimes you may have to reverse-engineer a SET-UP WANT later in order to find one that works with both the POINT OF NO RETURN and the CRISIS or TRIUMPH.

When writers in my workshops begin applying the Nutshell Technique to their own stories, I tell them to fill in the SET-UP WANT last. Even if they think they know it, I tell them to skip it and fill out the other seven elements on the Nutshell Technique form first. I urge you to follow this advice, too, when you are developing your story Nutshells. We can always find a SET-UP WANT later that works with the POINT OF NO RETURN and the CRISIS/TRIUMPH.

Your protagonist will have many wants. The SET-UP WANT is not necessarily the first one that comes to your mind, nor is it necessarily the thing the protagonist wants the most. Your protagonist can still want lots of other things that they don't get. But in order for the Nutshell Technique to work in helping you properly set up a story, you need to identify a SET-

UP WANT, one thing your protagonist wants that they actually get in the POINT OF NO RETURN, and you have to show it in your protagonist's first scene.

Don't mistake the SET-UP WANT for your protagonist's deeper, overall "want," or their motivation or overall objective as a character. The SET-UP WANT may or may not be the same as these deeper wants. Sometimes your SET-UP WANT is what I call a "throwaway WANT," and that's perfectly okay. Let me give you two examples.

If writers come to my workshop and don't already have a story to write in mind, I have them look through newspapers with crime stories and start building a story Nutshell around one of these. In the newspaper, you can find lots of seeds to begin a story: people with obvious FLAWs, lots of POINTs OF NO RETURN, and so forth, and that's a rich place to start building a Nutshell. One such writer in one of my workshops found an article in the newspaper about a policewoman whose son came with her in her squad car on an overnight ride-along. That night while trying to apprehend a suspect, the policewoman and her partner engaged in gunfire, and her son was killed in the cross fire. This writer felt the POINT OF NO RETURN for her policewoman protagonist was: her son comes on a ride-along and is killed. It certainly does sound like one. It's hard to think of a bigger turning point in an entire lifetime than the death of your own child.

But the writer was puzzled. What could the policewoman possibly have wanted that she got in this POINT OF NO RETURN? She thought this wasn't going to work as a story because she couldn't imagine a SET-UP WANT that the protagonist got in the POINT OF NO RETURN. Another writer threw this out as a possible SET-UP WANT: for her son to appreciate what she does for a living. This would work! In the POINT OF NO RETURN (her son comes on a ride-along and is killed), she gets her WANT (for her son to appreciate what she does for a living) but with a big CATCH: her son is dead. She certainly didn't want her son to be killed, but that's the point of the CATCH: the protagonist gets something they WANT but they also get something else that they *don't* want. Jason Bourne wants to know who he is, but when he finds out, he doesn't like the answer. The policewoman's son finally sees what she does for a living, but now he's dead and she no longer has a son. The protagonist gets their SET-UP WANT, but there's always a big CATCH.

[59]

We could even be more twisted with the policewoman story. We could have an opening scene where our protagonist and her son are having an argument, as mothers and sons do all the time, and in the scene she screams to her son, "Just shut up! Would you shut up for once?!" Here the SET-UP WANT would be: for her son to shut up. Same POINT OF NO RETURN (her son comes on a ride-along and is killed). A moment of anger prompted a wish for her son to "just shut up." It's a throwaway line, something the audience is not supposed to take seriously. Does she get her WANT? Yes, he shut up, all right! So, are we suggesting that she wanted him dead? No, of course not! She wanted him to shut up, but she never would have said it if she knew her wish would come true by him being killed. She gets her WANT but with a big, horrible CATCH attached to it.

Another great example of a "throwaway WANT" is in *Groundhog Day*. The POINT OF NO RETURN for Phil the weatherman is that he wakes up and it's Groundhog Day again: the day won't move forward, at 18–25%: 0:18:18–0:25:10 (notice also how the POINT OF NO RETURN is reflected in the film's title: February 2, Groundhog Day, is the day he gets "stuck" on). The whole second act is Phil trying to break out of this cycle. In reading the screenplay, I noticed a subtle but critical difference between what's written on the page in the first scene and what happens in the actual film.

In fact there are two very interesting differences between the screenplay and the actual film in the first scene. First, it's a story that involves the supernatural in some way—he keeps repeating the same day over and over—and yet no explanation is ever given for how this came to be. This is somewhat unusual. Typically in a movie when there is some kind of magic or supernatural occurrence the audience is given an explanation of how this came about.

No explanation is given in the film *Groundhog Day*, but in the original screenplay, the reader is given an explanation of how this magical event came to happen to him. In the January 7, 1992, draft,[1] credited as "by Danny Rubin Second Revision by Harold Ramis" (Ramis was the film's director and the eventually credited co-writer of an original spec script by Danny Rubin), Phil gets in an argument with Stephanie, an anchorwoman at his station he's been dating and who is mad he won't commit to her. Later we see her pull out a spell book and put the curse on him that causes him to have to repeat the same day over and over.

I don't know if these missing scenes were cut from the script before production began or if they actually shot them and ended up editing them out in postproduction, but at some point someone realized the audience didn't need the explanation of how the magic came to happen, and the Stephanie character, in fact, isn't in the film at all. Frankly, the explanation as written in this script version was clichéd and kind of cheesy. I wonder if the film would have the classic status it does today if this bit hadn't been cut, despite the fact that as an audience, we generally expect the origins of any magic to be explained to us.

The second significant difference between the first scene in the screenplay and the actual film is that the screenplay is missing a SET-UP WANT, but the film is not. The filmmakers didn't have the benefit of me there on the set to tell them, "Hey, guys—you forgot the SET-UP WANT!" But somewhere somewhat late in the process they obviously realized for themselves that something was missing.

In the scene, Phil is about to leave for his annual trip to Punxsutawney, where he covers the emergence of the groundhog, and he's talking with the substitute weatherman who is going to fill in for Phil while he's away. In the actual film, but not in any of the screenplay versions I've seen, the substitute weatherman is sucking up to Phil. He tells Phil to feel free to take his time in Punxsutawney and to spend another night if he wants to, because the substitute will be happy to cover for him for as long as Phil wants (because then the substitute will get more on-air time). Phil replies, "C'mon, I wanna stay an extra second in Punxsutawney?! Please!" So how could we state Phil's first-scene SET-UP WANT? To spend no more than 24 hours in Punxsutawney. In the POINT OF NO RETURN (the day won't move forward), does Phil get this WANT? Yes, he gets exactly that—not to spend more than 24 hours in Punxsutawney—but with a big CATCH attached: he keeps reliving the same 24 hours, indefinitely.

For those viewers who noticed that this magical event was never explained, it was probably a fleeting occurrence, and the thought was soon forgotten. Knowing the particularities behind the magic just isn't important. We can accept this relatively easily in our suspension of disbelief. But, interestingly, what the filmmakers correctly sensed was that we *did* need to know that Phil *asked for* this magical event. He wished it upon himself. He arrogantly proclaims that Punxsutawney is so awful that he will only spend 24 hours there. Be careful what you wish for!

[61]

The SET-UP WANT on the Nutshell Technique form is not necessarily the protagonist's big underlying "want" or their all-encompassing motivation. Characters, just like people, want lots of things. If I were the actor playing the part of Phil and I was trying to figure out what Phil wants from an acting point of view—in other words, what my intentions or objectives were as the actor playing the character of Phil—I'd focus in on the fact that Phil says that a major network is interested in him and he thinks this station is beneath him. I'd also focus on how he thinks he's God's gift to women, and yet women don't seem to fall for his "charm." He desires a network job; he wishes women worshipped him; all these "wants" are valid. But none of them are the Nutshell SET-UP WANT, because he doesn't get any of them in the POINT OF NO RETURN.

Let me define more specifically what constitutes the protagonist's first scene. By "scene" I don't mean the most literal sense of the word: that is, only from one scene header to a second scene header in the screenplay. I'm referring to the colloquial, common usage of the word. When we speak about a scene in a film, we're really talking about a "beat," which refers to one event, or one through-line of action, that often takes place over a couple of scene headers before it is complete.[2]

For example, the "scene" in *The Bourne Identity* where Bourne goes to the bank and opens up his safe-deposit box isn't technically one scene if you look at the actual script.[3] There are seven scene headers for this one beat of action to be complete:

1. EXT. ZURICH BANK—DAY: Bourne eyes the bank from across the street.
2. INT. ZURICH BANK/RECEPTION AREA—DAY: Bourne tells the receptionist he's here about a numbered account.
3. INT. ZURICH BANK/SECURITY CHECKPOINT—DAY: A bank guard guides his hand through a biometric scanner.
4. INT. ZURICH BANK/HALLWAY—DAY: A guard leads him to a special elevator.
5. INT. ZURICH BANK/VAULT ROOM—DAY: The elevator opens and another man escorts him down a corridor.
6. INT. ZURICH BANK/VAULT ROOM—DAY: A guard places the safety deposit box on a table before him and then leaves him in privacy. Bourne opens the box and discovers its contents.

7. INT. ZURICH BANK/VAULT ROOM—DAY: Bourne hands the box back to a guard.

When you watch a film and try to determine the protagonist's SET-UP WANT, you really want to watch and listen for the protagonist's first scene that contains dialogue. If the film has opening credits, they sometimes run over a montage or other non-dialogue scenes, and typically an opening montage isn't a good source to find the SET-UP WANT. Ideally we need to hear the protagonist speak. The protagonist does not always say directly what the SET-UP WANT is, but we do need to get a better sense of the protagonist than we typically get in a no-dialogue credits montage.

In *Collateral*, the SET-UP WANT is in what I consider to be the protagonist's first real dialogue scene, although technically there are five scene headers in the screenplay between when we first hear protagonist Max (Jamie Foxx) speak until when the SET-UP WANT is established. Here are those five scene headers as written in the screenplay[4] with a description of what is said and done in each scene from the actual film:

1. EXT/INT. CAB—GAS STATION—LATE DAY: Max, beginning his shift as an LA cab driver, talks with a gas station attendant in Spanish (it is not subtitled).
2. INT. CAB—MAGIC HOUR—SUPERIOR COURT BUILDING: Max sees a potential client, Annie (Jada Pinkett Smith), talking on her cell phone.
3. EXT./INT. CAB: Annie gets in his cab, and they make a bet on the fastest route to get to her destination
4. EXT. OLYMPIC BLVD.—DUSK TO NIGHT: There is no dialogue. We just watch him cruise through the quiet streets of the quicker route he chose.
5. INT. CAB—DUSK TO NIGHT: He's won the bet. She asks how long he's been a cab driver. He says that being a cabbie is just a temporary thing while he's putting together a luxury limo business. It'll be so nice, he says: "When you get to the airport, you're not going to want to get out."

The SET-UP WANT is established in the scene after the fifth scene header, although I would still call this the protagonist's first dialogue scene. The dialogue in the scene after the first scene header is in Spanish and is not subtitled, which deliberately makes it incomprehensible for a portion of the

[63]

audience. This scene is also at the tail end of an otherwise no-dialogue montage of him beginning his shift, and as I've mentioned, montages are not good sources for determining the SET-UP WANT. The scene after the second scene header has only the Annie character speaking as Max watches. Then after the third scene header, Max and Annie make a bet, which makes this the first dialogue spoken by Max that non-Spanish speakers can understand. The scene after the fourth scene header has no dialogue, and the scene after the fifth header is really a continuation of the conversation after scene header three, as they establish that Max won the bet.

In these five scenes, the script and the actual film are close to identical, with the conspicuous exception of the last line of dialogue I quoted about the customer not wanting to get out of his car. It's not in the screenplay; it's just in the film. And guess what? It contains the SET-UP WANT, which I think goes to show that if you omit the protagonist's SET-UP WANT, the filmmakers will probably rewrite your script to include one anyway.

So what is Max's SET-UP WANT? <u>For the passenger to not want to leave his car</u>. Every protagonist wants multiple things, but only one want is the SET-UP WANT. In this same scene, for example, Max wants the courage to ask Annie out on a date, as evidenced by when she leaves the cab and he shakes his head and sighs at his ineptitude in not having asked her out. But in the SET-UP WANT we're looking for a WANT that he *gets* in the POINT OF NO RETURN. So what's the POINT OF NO RETURN? When is Max in a situation where a passenger doesn't want to leave his car? If you've seen the film, surely you'll recognize that he gets this in the POINT OF NO RETURN when <u>Vincent</u> (Tom Cruise) <u>hires him to drive all night, and a body crashes on his cab</u> (14–18%: 0:17:00–0:21:40). The CATCH is <u>he's a hostage of a hired killer</u>.

So when you are establishing the SET-UP WANT, you have a bit of leeway as far as what constitutes the protagonist's first dialogue scene. That said, in most scripts the SET-UP WANT *will* be established after the very first scene header of the protagonist's first dialogue scene, as it is in the following films discussed thus far: *The Bourne Identity*, *Little Miss Sunshine*, *The Sixth Sense*, *The Usual Suspects*, and *Witness*. I'm surprised at how often the SET-UP WANT is somehow buried in that very first dialogue scene. These films tend to have more ironic story Nutshells because of it, and never forget that irony is a powerful tool for the writer.

Sometimes the SET-UP WANT can be quite subtle. That's because it's not necessarily the thing the protagonist wants the most; nor is it necessarily the thing that drives the protagonist's underlying motivations. Ultimately, the SET-UP WANT is simply the WANT in the first dialogue scene that works the *best* with the POINT OF NO RETURN and the CRISIS/TRIUMPH.

When I first attempted to Nutshell *Juno*, I couldn't find a strong SET-UP WANT in the very first scene that worked. Remember: to determine if I have the correct WANT, I need to know the POINT OF NO RETURN, so I identify the POINT OF NO RETURN first. The protagonist is Juno (Ellen Page), a 16-year-old who finds out she's pregnant. The POINT OF NO RETURN is when Juno's classmate Su-Chin is protesting outside an abortion clinic and tells her the fetus has fingernails. This really gets to her, and Juno finds she can't go through with the abortion she had planned to have. The POINT OF NO RETURN is told her fetus has fingernails, she can't go through with the abortion (18–20%: 0:16:36–0:19:25). Note also that the POINT OF NO RETURN is *not* "she discovers she's pregnant," which is, in fact, the Inciting Incident (see text box, page 44). That moment doesn't work as the POINT OF NO RETURN because (1) it happens way too early (at 0:05:34) and (2) it isn't a POINT OF NO RETURN where everything has changed in terms of what makes this movie *this* movie. Yes, her life is changed upon discovering she's pregnant, but what *really* changed everything and put this movie on course to be the movie we know as *Juno* is the POINT OF NO RETURN, when told her fetus has fingernails, she can't go through with the abortion. Had this not happened, Juno would have gone through with the abortion and returned to essentially her same life as a high school student, and the story would have been over. The movie *Juno* is not about what happens when a girl discovers she's pregnant; it's about what happens when a girl decides she can't go through with an abortion.

So what did Juno get in the POINT OF NO RETURN that she wanted in the first scene? In the very first scene, Juno is eyeing a set of living room furniture someone has left out on the curb for garbage pickup. She tells us in voiceover, "It started with a chair." I couldn't find a WANT in this scene that she got in the POINT OF NO RETURN. So I looked ahead a few scenes for the WANT. The next scene is a flashback of her having sex with her classmate Paulie, in a different chair. Next scene: we cut back to Juno on the curb considering the living room set again. She yells at a barking

[65]

dog and then tells us in voiceover, "This is the most magnificent discarded living room set I've ever seen." Then, there's a title sequence over music with Juno walking through an animated version of her town. Then, she's at the drugstore buying her third pregnancy test and using their bathroom to confirm her suspicions that she's pregnant.

The WANT I originally came up with was "to figure out what to do." Using a very loose interpretation of "first dialogue scene," I was identifying the WANT from the scene at the drugstore where she confirms she's pregnant and she's surely wondering what she was going to do next. Then in the POINT OF NO RETURN, she thinks she wants an abortion, but when Su-Chin comes along and mentions fingernails, she realizes she can't go through with it and instead decides she will put the baby up for adoption. Hence, she's figured out what to do; she got her WANT. Sort of . . .

A writer in one of my workshops came up with a much more clever SET-UP WANT than my "to figure out what to do," and, even better, it works with the very first dialogue scene: Juno's SET-UP WANT is to save something that is being discarded. Ah-ha! In the first scene as she stands by the curb, she wants to save the living room set; then in the POINT OF NO RE-TURN she decides not to "discard" the fetus she was about to abort.

Notice also how it's another example of a "throwaway WANT." It's not some deep "want" or intention or character motivation that Juno has under-neath, driving her behavior. We could say that Juno the character "wants" a number of things: respect, Paulie's friendship, to not be pregnant. But she doesn't get any of those things in the POINT OF NO RETURN. She may indeed desire these things, but none of them are the SET-UP WANT.

We're just looking for a WANT to set up "be careful what you wish for" in your story, and often that's nothing deep. I'm not saying that your pro-tagonist doesn't desire deep things. But right now we're just setting up the story. All Juno wants in the first dialogue scene is a set of living room furni-ture someone left at the curb. I tell my writers to consider that sometimes all your protagonist wants is a sandwich!

You do have a bit of flexibility in what you determine to be the first scene in which to display your protagonist's SET-UP WANT. It doesn't have to be after the very first scene header, but the closer the better. You defi-nitely don't want it to be beyond what would be considered the first beat of action for the protagonist. And you would be surprised how often the

What does Juno (Ellen Page) want in her first scene? Still from *Juno*. Copyright 2007, Twentieth Century Fox Film Corporation.

SET-UP WANT is, in fact, buried in that very first scene—and such films tend to have more clever, ironic stories because of it.

The SET-UP WANT is also the easiest element of the Nutshell to reverse-engineer, which is another reason why I urge you to fill it in on the Nutshell Technique form last and only after you fill in the other seven elements of the Nutshell. You really risk setting yourself up for failure if you start a story Nutshell by locking into one idea about what you think your protagonist's SET-UP WANT is. Then you are forced to create a POINT OF NO RETURN in which they *have to* get this initial WANT, and this will likely turn your story in an entirely different direction than you originally intended.

Let's pretend *Groundhog Day* was never written and therefore was never subsequently made into the classic film that it is. And let's pretend we are trying to write such a story from scratch. We start with our protagonist Phil, the obnoxious weatherman. What is his WANT? Well, the first thing that comes to my mind is that he wants "a big network job." That seems like a big part of who this character is: he thinks he's hot stuff and he's above everyone at this local TV station. If "a big network job" is his Nutshell SET-UP WANT, then he has to get this WANT in the POINT OF NO RETURN. Does he get "a big network job" in the POINT OF NO RETURN, when <u>the day won't move forward</u>? No, he doesn't get a big network job when this happens. So does this mean we need to create a different POINT OF NO RE-TURN in order to find one where he gets his desire for "a big network job"?

Well, we could do this, but it would significantly change the story. He could go to Punxsutawney and get spotted by a network and be offered a job. We could state the POINT OF NO RETURN as "a network offers him a job." He wanted a network job, he got a network job. So the Nutshell WANT/POINT OF NO RETURN relationship technically works. But is this script going to be anything like the classic we know as *Groundhog Day*? Our theoretical movie sounds like it's going to be about an obnoxious small-town weatherman getting hired for a big network job, and now he'll encounter some kind of difficulties at the job, and who knows where the story is going from there. It is nowhere close to the film we know as *Groundhog Day*. We absolutely have to have Phil experience the day won't move forward at some point or it just won't resemble anything like the classic that is the real *Groundhog Day*. I guess we could have the day won't move forward happen in addition to Phil getting the big network job, or before or after a new job happens, but the day won't move forward is so much more a true POINT OF NO RETURN. People get new jobs every day, but how often does it happen that the day won't move forward?

It is impossible to re-create the classic that is *Groundhog Day* without the POINT OF NO RETURN being the day won't move forward. It would end up being a completely different story. So what does this mean—does this mean Phil *doesn't* desire a big network job? No, he says a network is interested in him and he clearly wants this to happen. He desires lots of things, just like in life we all desire many things. But there is really only one POINT OF NO RETURN that truly makes any given story the story that it is.

It's much, much easier and more sensible to approach the WANT/POINT OF NO RETURN relationship from the other way around. First define your protagonist's POINT OF NO RETURN, *then* find (or invent) a SET-UP WANT in their first scene that they get in that POINT OF NO RETURN, and don't finalize the WANT until *last*, after you've determined all the other Nutshell elements.

Don't make the mistake of changing the POINT OF NO RETURN to work with a WANT you had in mind. Unfortunately, I see writers do this all the time: they fixate on something they know their protagonist really "wants" and get frustrated that it doesn't work with the POINT OF NO RETURN.

Then instead of looking for something else the protagonist wants that they actually get, they change the POINT OF NO RETURN. Bad idea. It should be the other way around—change the WANT to work with the POINT OF NO RETURN.

And it's important to remember that if your proposed WANT doesn't work because your protagonist doesn't get the WANT in the POINT OF NO RETURN, that doesn't mean that you have to rewrite the character so they don't "want" whatever you initially proposed. It just means that it's a "lowercase want." It's a "want" that they don't get and therefore it doesn't belong on the Nutshell Technique form, but the protagonist can still desire it. You just need to find *another* WANT that they *do* get in the POINT OF NO RETURN.

Only after you determine the POINT OF NO RETURN should you consider the SET-UP WANT. But at this point, I would still only pencil it in. After identifying the POINT OF NO RETURN, you need a sense of what the WANT is to evaluate whether the protagonist is getting something they wanted in the POINT OF NO RETURN and also to help determine what they got that they *didn't* want (the CATCH). But even now you need to stay flexible about your idea of what the WANT is, because the POINT OF NO RETURN isn't the only Nutshell element with which the WANT has to work properly. Very often you have to tweak or even change the WANT in order for it to work with the CRISIS/TRIUMPH, because the CRISIS must, in a comedy, be the opposite of the SET-UP WANT (in a tragedy we have a TRIUMPH, which is the ideal manifestation of the SET-UP WANT). We'll get into all the details about how the CRISIS and TRIUMPH work in Chapters 10 and 11, but I bring it up now to emphasize the importance of continuing to be flexible about what you think the SET-UP WANT is. Only when you get to the CRISIS/TRIUMPH will you be able to lock in your WANT.

I try to Nutshell every movie I see, but it's really hard to Nutshell a movie when you see it in the theater. When you stream a movie or watch a DVD, you can easily stop and replay a scene or even turn the English subtitles on, which can really help you focus on specific lines of dialogue. But when you see it in the theater, it is very difficult to Nutshell, and the hardest part to determine is always the SET-UP WANT. First, I have to guess who the protagonist is going to be, which is something you can't know with certainty for awhile (on rare occasions not until the very end of a movie).

[69]

Second, the WANT is contained in the very first moments in the film, and we usually don't understand exactly what we're seeing and hearing yet; we, the audience, are putting together the details and trying to grasp the relationships and behavior on display. If I watch a movie and think I know what the SET-UP WANT is based on what I've just seen and heard in the first beat, I might be right, but really I'm just guessing. I won't have a clue whether I'm right until I get to the POINT OF NO RETURN, when I would see the protagonist get this WANT. And I still wouldn't know definitively that I had the correct WANT, because the WANT also must, in a comedy, be the opposite of the CRISIS (in a tragedy, we have a TRIUMPH, which is the ultimate manifestation of the WANT), and the CRISIS/TRIUMPH doesn't occur until around 1:30:00 into the film. If I were to guess the SET-UP WANT based on the first scenes of the film, I'd probably guess whatever I perceive is the thing the protagonist desires the most, and, as I've discussed, the thing the protagonist desires the most is not necessarily the SET-UP WANT. The odds that this first guess of the SET-UP WANT in the first scene is going to end up working with the POINT OF NO RETURN at 25 minutes and with the CRISIS/TRIUMPH at 90 minutes are slim.

Rather than locking into a guess of what the protagonist seems to most want, what I do is scribble down a quick description of what is happening and bits of key dialogue in the first beat, or beats, if I don't have a good sense of who the protagonist is. Then I might venture a couple of guesses for the WANT. When I get to the POINT OF NO RETURN, I consider what the protagonist got out of it and whether I can express this as something they wanted in that first beat. Sometimes I can, sometimes I can't, but either way, I won't know I have the correct WANT until I get to the CRISIS/TRIUMPH and can see that the WANT and CRISIS are opposites, in the case of a comedy (or that the TRIUMPH is the ultimate manifestation of the WANT, if it's a tragedy). Very often I have to go back and read through that dialogue I scribbled down. Sometimes I can't see a connection between the WANT and the POINT OF NO RETURN, but when I get to the CRISIS and consider what the opposite of it is (or its ultimate manifestation in the TRIUMPH), *then* I can figure out the WANT.

[70]

Whether you are Nutshelling your own story or analyzing one for an existing film, the SET-UP WANT will always be the most difficult Nutshell element to determine and usually can't be identified until the rest of the Nut-shell elements start to fall into place. You can consider the possibilities after identifying the POINT OF NO RETURN, but only after the CRISIS or TRIUMPH has been determined can you know the SET-UP WANT with certainty.

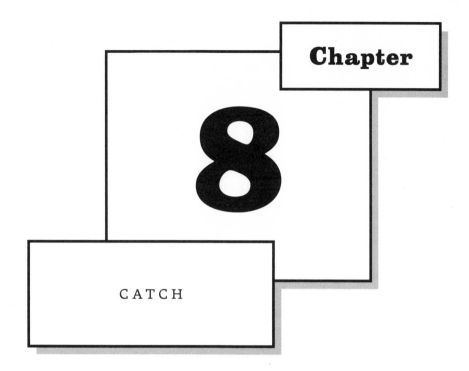

Chapter

8

CATCH

The **CATCH***:*

- comes directly and immediately as a part of the POINT OF NO RETURN
- is what the protagonist got in the POINT OF NO RETURN that they *didn't* want and should be self-evident at this point in the story
- will become the perfect test of the protagonist's FLAW

Also:

- it's the CATCH from the protagonist's point of view
- it comes as part of the POINT OF NO RETURN and is not a later complication
- it is in existence by page 30 or 0:30:00, since it is a part of the POINT OF NO RETURN

Film Nutshells Discussed in This Chapter

The Bourne Identity
Braveheart
Titanic

Tootsie
The Usual Suspects
Little Miss Sunshine
The Sixth Sense

ON THE NUTSHELL TECHNIQUE FORM, the CATCH is right below the POINT OF NO RETURN to alert you to the fact that the POINT OF NO RETURN and the CATCH are immediately and directly related. The POINT OF NO RETURN brings the protagonist what they wanted in the SET-UP WANT—but be careful what you wish for! In the POINT OF NO RETURN, they got their WANT, but they got it in an ironic sense. Simultaneous with getting something they wanted, the protagonist also gets something they *didn't* want, and that is the CATCH.

In *The Bourne Identity,* Jason Bourne gets his SET-UP WANT to figure out who he is in the POINT OF NO RETURN when a safe-deposit box reveals he's Jason Bourne and has multiple passports, a gun, and cash (14–15%: 0:15:57–0:18:21). He gets his WANT, but there's a CATCH: looks like he's a dangerous criminal.

The CATCH is not new information or a new event or complication that develops later in Act 2. The CATCH is attached directly to the POINT OF NO RETURN, and thus occurs before the break into Act 2. It is specifically from seeing the contents of the safe-deposit box that Bourne gets the information that it looks like he's a dangerous criminal, and from this point forward, he must face the world with this knowledge.

Ideally the POINT OF NO RETURN is expressed in such a way that the CATCH is self-evident. If you read only my POINT OF NO RETURN description for Bourne—a safe-deposit box reveals he's Jason Bourne and has multiple passports, a gun, and cash—you would surmise the CATCH for yourself. Multiple identities, a gun, and cash? That seems ominous; that sounds like the contents of a criminal's safe-deposit box, you might say.

You want to express the Nutshell Technique elements in as few words as possible on the form. This being the case, the CATCH may not always be self-evident from your description of the POINT OF NO RETURN. While it may not be self-evident on the form, the CATCH must be self-evident at this point in the story: that is, by the POINT OF NO RETURN in the screenplay or film.

Remember the example I gave of the writer in one of my workshops who started a Nutshell based on an article in the newspaper? The protagonist was a policewoman. The SET-UP WANT was either: for her son to appreciate what she does for a living or for her son to shut up. Either WANT would work at this stage because she gets both in the POINT OF NO RETURN: her son comes on a ride-along and is killed. Here the CATCH is self-evident: her son is dead. She got her WANT, but she also got something she very much didn't want.

The Nutshell for *Braveheart* works similarly. The Scottish men are going to battle the English, and protagonist William Wallace, age eight, tries to come with them. "I can fight," the youngster proclaims. His father agrees that the boy is capable of fighting, but he won't let him come, saying "It's our wits that make us men." The ability to fight isn't what makes a boy a man. A boy becomes a man when he has the brains to know *when* to fight, and you should only fight when you have a good reason. Young William's SET-UP WANT is a reason to fight, but his countrymen keep giving him reasons why he shouldn't. In the next beat, his uncle takes a sword away from the boy. "First learn to use this," his uncle says, tapping his temple. "Then I will teach you to use this," he says, lifting the sword. When adult William (played by Mel Gibson) tries to court Murron, his future wife, her father will allow him only if he promises to stay out of the rebel fighting that has begun brewing.

The POINT OF NO RETURN comes when his wife is murdered by the English (25%: 0:44:36–0:45:58). He now has his WANT, a reason to fight, and he leads the Scots into a full-scale rebellion against the British. What's the CATCH? This one should be self-evident. He got his WANT (a reason to fight) in the POINT OF NO RETURN when his wife is murdered by the English, but what did he get that he didn't want? The terrible CATCH is his wife is dead.

If we were to read the SET-UP WANT and POINT OF NO RETURN statements on the Nutshell Technique form, ideally the CATCH would be self-evident as the thing the protagonist got that they *didn't* want, as it was in the two examples I just gave, but sometimes it's more evident than other times.

In *Titanic*, the POINT OF NO RETURN for protagonist Rose is she falls overboard, but Jack saves her (20–23%: 0:38:16–0:43:56). This gives her

her SET-UP WANT, which is to go overboard (because she was suicidal and thought of *Titanic* as a slave ship transporting her to a wedding in which she didn't want to participate). What is the CATCH? It is not as self-evident as in my previous examples. The CATCH is she meets Jack. The POINT OF NO RETURN and its CATCH are the last things that happen in Act 1, when the world was black and white, and signal our entry into the Technicolor land of Act 2, where our protagonist embarks on a new adventure. For Rose, her adventure really begins when she meets Jack. From that moment on, everything has changed as they keep finding themselves drawn to each other and their fates begin to intertwine. While it's not as obvious a CATCH as the death of a loved one, when she meets Jack is the beginning of her *real* story and of her ultimate transformation from someone whose FLAW is cowardice into someone who gains in the end the STRENGTH of bravery.

One of the purposes of the CATCH is to front-load your second act with an immediate problem for your protagonist. In the POINT OF NO RETURN, your protagonist got their SET-UP WANT, which means that without a CATCH (which is a new problem for your protagonist), you have removed a major conflict (wanting the WANT). No conflict means no drama, and drama is an essential requirement for maintaining dramatic stories (which is what all screenplays are). Your story is over—unless there's a CATCH.

The CATCH, however, isn't new information or a new event or a new complication that develops later in Act 2. It comes immediately and directly as a result of the POINT OF NO RETURN. Think of the CATCH as me questioning you: in the POINT OF NO RETURN, your protagonist got their SET-UP WANT, but what did they get that they *didn't* want? If that doesn't give you your CATCH, let me ask you two follow-up questions: as we begin Act 2, why isn't the story over now? What's your protagonist's problem now? Because if there's no problem, there's no conflict, and your story is over.

From the protagonist's perspective, the CATCH poses an immediate problem but not an insurmountable one. In *Tootsie*, protagonist Michael Dorsey (Dustin Hoffman) is an out-of-work actor, desperate for an acting job. His SET-UP WANT is a job. He gets one in the POINT OF NO RETURN— he auditions disguised as a woman for a female role, and gets the part—

a soap opera role is offered to Michael (22%: 0:25:19–0:25:23). The CATCH is he must pretend to be a woman, and Michael practically boasts to his roommate that the CATCH is giving him one of the greatest challenges for an actor. He makes the CATCH sound like a good thing! The protagonist might try to pass off the CATCH as a positive, but it should be obvious to the audience that it is truly a problem for them. Michael may act like he relishes the opportunity, but we know he would much prefer an acting job where he didn't have to do all he has to do to pass himself off as a woman.

There are two realizations in most stories that one might call "catches," but only one of these is the correct CATCH for the Nutshell Technique form. What writers occasionally identify incorrectly as their Nutshell CATCH is something that actually resembles the correct Nutshell STRENGTH for their protagonist in the end. It would be as if we said, incorrectly, that the CATCH for *Tootsie*'s Michael was "he discovers that 'walking in a woman's shoes' isn't very pleasant." That statement is actually close to stating what STRENGTH he gains in the very end, which is respect for women from his experience of having walked literally in a woman's shoes.

The Nutshell CATCH, however, is something that happens to your protagonist along with the POINT OF NO RETURN and thus before the break into Act 2, although the CATCH will ultimately lead the protagonist to the STRENGTH in the very end in an Aristotelian comedy (I'll address the CATCH in a tragedy shortly). As they enter Act 2, the protagonist perceives their biggest problem at this point to be the CATCH. At the beginning of Act 2, Michael thinks his problem is he must pretend to be a woman. Every ounce of his energy in Act 2 is directed toward maintaining this secret. But by the end of Act 2, Michael's problem isn't that he has to pretend to be a woman. As a matter of fact, he does such a good job of it that, astonishingly, not one person has figured out he's really a man. The CATCH has distracted him from seeing his real problem, which is his own FLAW: he doesn't respect women. He has been so busy pretending to be a woman that he didn't even realize that the CATCH contained the ideal test of his FLAW. It is from the experience of literally walking in a woman's shoes that he begins his transformation toward the STRENGTH he gains in the very end: respect for women.

In the POINT OF NO RETURN the protagonist got their SET-UP WANT,

[77]

so now the screenwriter must make sure they don't enjoy that fact by making sure a CATCH is attached to the POINT OF NO RETURN that will be the ideal test of their FLAW. The CATCH will be the primary source of the obstacles that you, the screenwriter, will be throwing in your protagonist's path throughout Act 2.

Almost all of the obstacles in *Tootsie*'s second act originate from the CATCH that he must pretend to be a woman:

- Dressed in his female persona of Dorothy Michaels, he accosts his agent at the Russian Tea Room and successfully fools him into believing Michael is a woman.
- Michael reveals to his agent he's actually Michael, and his agent begs him to get therapy. Michael explains he got the female soap opera role, but now he needs some cash.
- He buys a woman's wardrobe but frets that he still doesn't have a good handbag. He plans strategies for makeup and how to keep his 5 o'clock shadow at bay.
- With the high-paying soap gig, he now has the cash he needs to produce his roommate's play, but he has to lie to Sandy (Teri Garr) about how he got it, and so he tells her he got the money when an aunt died.
- He sneaks and tries on some of Sandy's clothes, and when she catches him in her bedroom in only his underwear, he pretends he undressed because he wants to seduce her, and they end up having sex.
- Sandy is anxious that now he's never going to call her, so he commits to a dinner date the next evening despite his insane schedule.

All of these complications came out of the CATCH that he must pretend to be a woman, and these were in just the first six minutes of Act 2! A good CATCH will be the source of endless fodder to test your protagonist and their FLAW. You need a CATCH that can provide a relentless assault against your protagonist due to their FLAW, because that's essentially what Act 2 is all about: the protagonist's FLAW constantly butting up against complications that come out of or follow from the CATCH.

You may have noticed that the Nutshell Technique focuses on elements that are mostly in Act 1 (the SET-UP WANT, the POINT OF NO RETURN, and the CATCH) and in Act 3 (the CLIMACTIC CHOICE and the FINAL STEP).

If these elements in your beginning and your end are set up properly, they do most of the structural work of supporting the middle that is Act 2. Act 2 is twice as long as the other acts, yet on the Nutshell Technique form, the only elements that directly correlate to it are the CATCH (which actually takes place as part of the POINT OF NO RETURN and is therefore in Act 1; the CATCH, however, contains what will be the perfect test of the FLAW in Act 2); the CRISIS or TRIUMPH (which happen at the very end of Act 2); and the FLAW. The FLAW doesn't actually take place in a fixed moment in time. The protagonist's FLAW existed before the story began. We'll see hints of it throughout Act 1, but in Act 2, the FLAW really comes into play.

The CATCH is a part of the POINT OF NO RETURN and therefore is revealed at the end of Act 1, but it needs to indicate an ideal test of the FLAW, and enough of one that we can believe that the conflict between the CATCH and the protagonist's FLAW will sustain itself and drive all of Act 2. Eventually, the CATCH and the FLAW will lead directly to the CRISIS or TRIUMPH at the end of Act 2. At the CRISIS in a comedy, the protagonist will be in exactly the opposite state of mind that they were in at the SET-UP WANT (in a tragedy the TRIUMPH will take them to the ultimate manifestation of the SET-UP WANT). So in a comedy the CATCH is the beginning of a transformation in the protagonist that will usually lead them to hate their initial SET-UP WANT (in a tragedy the CATCH will further their love of the SET-UP WANT). In a comedy the CATCH will typically make the WANT become something undesirable, and the protagonist will usually abandon the WANT (in a tragedy, the CATCH will further the protagonist's desire for the WANT, and they'll often ultimately be destroyed by it).

In *Tootsie*, the progression looks like this:

SET-UP WANT:	job
POINT OF NO RETURN:	a soap opera role is offered to Michael
CATCH:	he must pretend to be a woman
FLAW:	doesn't respect women
CRISIS:	wants *out* of the job

The CATCH for Michael that he must pretend to be a woman is the perfect test of his FLAW that he doesn't respect women. These two elements sum up the essence of Act 2. Throughout Act 2 he is either in disguise as a woman or hiding the fact that he has been in disguise; or else he is trying to use information he gleaned from being in disguise to further his interests. His FLAW that he doesn't respect women is constantly being challenged as he directly experiences just how it feels to be a woman being mistreated by men, and yet he continues to lie to and mistreat the women in his life. This will lead him lower and lower until he reaches his lowest point in the story, the CRISIS, where he hates his situation so much that he wants out of the job that at the beginning of the story he so desperately coveted.

In a tragedy, the CATCH also provides the perfect opportunity for change but, in this case, the protagonist fails to change from their FLAW, and they fail to gain the STRENGTH. Instead of the CATCH leading the protagonist to the CRISIS at the end of Act 2, which would be their lowest point and the opposite of their WANT in a comedy, in a tragedy the CATCH will further their love of the WANT and lead them to their TRIUMPH, which is their highest point and the ultimate manifestation of their WANT.

In *The Usual Suspects*, the tragic progression for the protagonist, customs agent Kujan, looks like this:

SET-UP WANT:	to see Keaton go down
POINT OF NO RETURN:	the police sergeant lets him talk to Verbal
CATCH:	Verbal is a physically challenged simpleton with total immunity
FLAW:	arrogant
TRIUMPH:	proves to Verbal that Keaton is Keyser Soze

The TRIUMPH, however, is only experienced briefly, because *The Usual Suspects* is a tragedy, which means Agent Kujan doesn't overcome his FLAW of being arrogant. It was arrogance that made him think he'd solved the mystery and reached his TRIUMPH, and he will make an arrogant CLIMACTIC CHOICE: he lets Verbal leave. As Verbal straightens his supposedly crippled legs and gets into an awaiting getaway car, Agent Kujan makes one desperate FINAL STEP and runs after him but it's too late.

[80]   The CATCH, that he believes Verbal is a physically challenged simpleton with total immunity, is his test throughout Act 2 and, due to his FLAW of being arrogant, he is blind to the fact that Verbal isn't spilling the beans; he's spinning a great yarn using objects Verbal spies in the very office

in which the interrogation takes place. Kujan arrogantly thinks he's triumphed in proving his case, only to discover, too late, that Verbal made the whole thing up.

So in a tragedy, the CATCH is the beginning of a transformation in the protagonist that will further their love of the SET-UP WANT, only to lead to their destruction in the very end of the story by the WANT. In *The Usual Suspects* the CATCH that Verbal is a physically challenged simpleton with total immunity feeds right into Agent Kujan's obsessive WANT, to see Keaton go down. Perceiving Verbal as a simpleton, obsessed with seeing Keaton go down, and aided in no small part by Verbal's skillful storytelling, Kujan thinks he's not only achieved his SET-UP WANT, to see Keaton go down, but that he's solved Verbal's mystery regarding the identity of Keyser Soze. Keaton was Keyser Soze and he used Verbal, Kujan proclaims. His obsession with Keaton blinds him to the fact that Keyser Soze is probably nothing more than Verbal's creation, and tragically, Kujan lets this criminal mastermind go free, only to realize what he has done too late.

Having a strong CATCH attached to your POINT OF NO RETURN is critical for setting up a story correctly. In it, you are front-loading your Act 2 with an immediate problem for your protagonist and one that is a direct challenge to their specific FLAW. If you don't have a CATCH testing a central FLAW, Act 2 ends up becoming a series of more-or-less random occurrences and meandering events, and it results in the writer presenting a situation instead of a story.

If possible, you should word the POINT OF NO RETURN so that the CATCH is self-evident. This is to ensure that your CATCH is not a new development or something that happens later in Act 2 but is instead something that came into existence as a part of the POINT OF NO RETURN. If the CATCH is not self-evident from reading only your WANT and POINT OF NO RETURN statements, it definitely would be self-evident if we read your actual script through just Act 1, which ends in the POINT OF NO RETURN and its CATCH.

In *Little Miss Sunshine*, protagonist Richard has a SET-UP WANT of a winner (in his first scene, he is giving his "the world is made up of winners and losers" motivational speech to a handful of people).

The POINT OF NO RETURN is when Olive gets into a pageant and tells Richard she'll win (17–20%: 0:16:45–0:21:05). Richard thus gets his WANT

[81]

(a winner), but what's the CATCH? It's not self-evident from just my WANT and POINT OF NO RETURN statements, but it would be if you had watched the film up to this point, or even if you watched just the POINT OF NO RETURN in the film. Let me describe the complete sequence of events that happens during the POINT OF NO RETURN (0:16:45–0:21:05):

- There is a message on their answering machine that says that their young daughter, Olive, got into a beauty pageant in California.
- Richard and his wife Sheryl argue about the fact that they can't afford to go because all their money is tied up in his inspirational program.
- Flying is out of the question financially, but if they drive, it turns out, due to a number of complications in their lives, the whole nutty family will have to come along, completely filling up their old VW bus.
- Richard tells Olive that there's no point in entering a contest unless you believe you're going to win (this is the philosophy behind his inspirational program). "Are you going to win?" he asks her. "Yes!" she replies, resoundingly, and Richard has his winner.

The CATCH is not going to be self-evident from just the SET-UP WANT and POINT OF NO RETURN descriptions I wrote, but if you watch 0:16:45–0:21:05 of the film, it will be self-evident to you. Because in between Olive gets into pageant and she tells Richard she'll win, the family first debates whether they can even afford to get her to the pageant, and they finally agree that they can, but it will require driving and the whole family coming along. And that is the CATCH: the whole crazy family has to drive her to California.

When you fill out the Nutshell Technique form for your own stories, make sure that the CATCH is either self-evident for someone reading the SET-UP WANT and the POINT OF NO RETURN statements, or, if it is not self-evident from the form, that it would be at this point in your script: that is, by the end of Act 1 (around pages 25–30).

The CATCH should be from the protagonist's point of view at the time of the POINT OF NO RETURN. On the Nutshell Technique form, you should state everything in the third person. Even if you were writing an autobiographical story, you would state the protagonist and the Nutshell statements in the third person. But make sure that the CATCH statement reflects what the protagonist would say is the CATCH, and not something the readers or viewers know that the protagonist doesn't know. In *The Sixth Sense*, protagonist Dr. Malcom Crowe's SET-UP WANT is to help kids in the most difficult situations. The POINT OF NO RETURN is Cole becomes his second chance. So what's the CATCH at this point?

It's not "Malcolm is killed" or "Malcolm's actually a ghost." At the time of the POINT OF NO RETURN, Malcolm doesn't know he's dead, so this is not the CATCH from his point of view (the audience doesn't know at this point either; only those watching the film a second time know he's a ghost). It's also not "Cole sees dead people," because Malcolm doesn't find out about this until 0:50:26.

In the same scene where Cole becomes his second chance (their first therapy session), Cole tells him, "You're nice, but you can't help me." From Malcolm's point of view the CATCH is Cole has no faith in him. Cole gives him a second chance to achieve his SET-UP WANT to help kids in the most difficult situations after he has failed another patient, but Malcolm will have his work cut out for him because of the CATCH that Cole has no faith in him. This CATCH is the perfect test of Malcolm's FLAW because Malcolm also lacks faith in himself.

Having a strong CATCH is essential for ensuring that your protagonist faces an immediate challenge as they enter Act 2. A good CATCH is needed to make a story great.

Let me leave you with an e-mail that a writer in one of my workshops sent me. He wrote to let me know that he wasn't able to make that evening's meeting because he was getting over a stomach virus. "But now I finally understand how the CATCH works," he wrote. "Recently, my WANT was: to lose a little weight. I got my WANT in this POINT OF NO RETURN: a stomach virus infected me, and I lost five pounds. The CATCH? Being sick is no fun!"

Chapter

9

FLAW

The **FLAW**:

- is one single FLAW, stated preferably in universal terms
- must be something over which the protagonist has control
- is what the CATCH tests and should be evident throughout Act 1 and especially Act 2

In a comedy:

- the FLAW is the direct opposite of what the protagonist learns in the end, the STRENGTH
- in both the CLIMACTIC CHOICE and the FINAL STEP, the protagonist will move away from the FLAW and toward the STRENGTH

In a tragedy:

- the FLAW is the direct opposite of the what the protagonist *fails to learn* in the end, the STRENGTH
- in both the CLIMACTIC CHOICE and the FINAL STEP, the protagonist will *fail to* move away from the FLAW and toward the STRENGTH

Film Nutshells Discussed in This Chapter

Tootsie
North Country
Being John Malkovich
The Bourne Identity
Argo
Witness

IN LIFE, WE ALL HAVE strengths and weaknesses. Well-developed fictional characters should have both, too. And your protagonist should have one weakness in particular—one specific personal FLAW—which they are going to have to face before the end of your story.

Your protagonist's FLAW may be the single most important element of the Nutshell, because it contains the source code for your whole story. It's not something that you easily can tack onto your script as an afterthought. The protagonist's FLAW *is* the story. This FLAW and how your protagonist deals with it are actually *what your story is secretly about.* Yet sometimes I see screenwriters leave it out altogether.

I was called in as a consultant on a script for a film that was to begin shooting in two weeks. They hoped I had a quick fix, but the script was in bad shape. I recommended halting production so a complete rewrite could be done. The story was about a true-life historical event that the executive producer was an expert on, but he was also a first-time filmmaker. I told him I wasn't sure how to advise him on how to approach the rewrite, because I couldn't get a good handle on the story they were trying to tell. For starters, I told him, I couldn't figure out what the protagonist's FLAW was. The executive producer piped up immediately and said that's easy. The flaw is that this other guy screwed up, and they didn't have enough ammo. No, I said. The FLAW isn't something someone else does. I'm asking what's the *protagonist's* FLAW. I have to understand the protagonist's FLAW if I'm going to understand the story you're trying to tell.

[86] Not being a writer, the executive producer had never considered this concept, so he gave it some thought. Only after we established what the protagonist's FLAW was could I help shape the rewrite so it would tell a satisfying story. The protagonist must have a FLAW; without a protago-

nist's FLAW at the heart of it, your plot will be just a bunch of random stuff happening to the protagonist. But it shouldn't be. Almost everything that happens in Act 2 is going to be an obstacle to your protagonist specifically because of their FLAW. The FLAW is the seed out of which your entire story sprouts.

You could say that *The Wizard of Oz* (not Nutshelled) is about a Kansas farm girl who wakes up in the magical Land of Oz and, to get back home, she has to follow a road through scary places so she can talk to a wizard she's told can help her. But it turns out that she alone has the power to bring herself home, which she does by proclaiming "there's no place like home." That's the *plot*.

But what *The Wizard of Oz* is really about is a girl whose FLAW is: she runs from problems instead of facing them. She tries to run away from home and ends up waking up in a land far away. Here she finds she has all new problems that are even scarier than the ones she was trying to escape. When she finally is able to return home, she is so relieved to be back that she promises that she'll never look for excitement further than her own backyard, because somewhere new won't take away your problems; it'll just make them worse. That's the *story*.

The plot is the sequence of events that moves the narrative forward. The story is the emotional journey and inner change that the protagonist undergoes in a comedy, or fails to undergo in a tragedy. When you think about it, so many film plots revolve around a physical journey. It's a great metaphor to use because, at the heart of it, all great stories are showing us an emotional journey. But if you don't give your protagonist a real FLAW to tackle, you're giving them no place to go.

As I discussed in Chapter 8 ("Catch"), Act 2 is largely driven by obstacles that come out of the conflict between the CATCH and the protagonist's FLAW. So when you use the Nutshell Technique form, you'll want to consider whether the FLAW you state sounds like something that could be so tested by your CATCH that it would sustain the entire 60 pages that typically make up Act 2. Ideally, you would say your CATCH is the *perfect* test of the FLAW.

The Nutshell Technique form isn't 100% about the story's chronology. While most of the Nutshell Technique elements correlate chronologically to specific points in the script or in the film's running time, the FLAW and the STRENGTH don't. The FLAW existed in the protagonist before the story began, and we should get a hint of it in the protagonist's very first scene and throughout Act 1.

Keep in mind that, just as characters all "want" more than one thing, so characters also have multiple flaws. *Tootsie's* Michael Dorsey hasn't been getting acting work, his agent tells him, because he's too difficult to work with. That may be his greatest flaw: "difficult." But it's not the Nutshell FLAW. Because the Nutshell FLAW—the FLAW that is the structural corner-stone of the story—is the one that the protagonist must grapple with; in a comedy, they will do a complete about-face on the FLAW by the end of the story and will learn its opposite, the STRENGTH (in a tragedy the pro-tagonist fails to change from the FLAW and learn its opposite STRENGTH). At the end of *Tootsie*, a comedy, I see no evidence that Michael will be any less difficult to work with on his next acting job. This flaw is still part of his character at the end of the story, and so it is not the Nutshell FLAW.

The Nutshell FLAW is not necessarily the protagonist's greatest flaw. The Nutshell FLAW is the one that's being tested by the CATCH; the pro-tagonist's interaction with this FLAW will lead them either to change and learn the STRENGTH (comedy), or to fail to change (tragedy).

What is Michael's Nutshell FLAW, the one the CATCH, he must pre-tend to be a woman, tests? Michael's FLAW is he doesn't respect women. Having to pretend to be a woman is the perfect test for a man who doesn't respect women. From literally walking in a woman's shoes he will see for himself how poorly men like him treat women. This will lead him to change in Act 3. In a comedy, in the CLIMACTIC CHOICE and the FINAL STEP the protagonist will make two distinct moves away from their FLAW and toward the STRENGTH. Michael's two steps away from his FLAW, doesn't respect women, and toward his STRENGTH, respect for women, in Act 3 are (1) his CLIMACTIC CHOICE: live on the air, he reveals he's a man and (2) his FINAL STEP: he tells Julie he's changed and learned to be a better man. By the end he's changed 180 degrees into a man who has the STRENGTH of respect for women.

[88]   The FLAW of doesn't respect women, which isn't even Michael's most prominent flaw, contains the DNA of the whole story. If he hadn't had this FLAW, the story wouldn't have worked. In fact, that was exactly the prob-lem with the original script. Director Sydney Pollack turned down doing

the film "at least six times. Because I thought it was a terrible script," as he said in an interview aired in the *On Story* television series.[1] The original script wasn't *about* anything, he said. It was just a one-joke story about a guy running around in drag pretending to be a woman, because the FLAW that he <u>doesn't respect women</u> wasn't in the original script. At one point Michael's agent has this line of dialogue: "Being a woman has made you weird." Pollack said, "And it suddenly occurred to me that if that line was 'being a woman has made a *man* out of you' that we would have something to make the movie about." It was then that Pollack knew exactly how to shape the rewrite. "You have to make him a bad man but you have to make him a bad man in the precise ways that could be illuminated by being a woman so that he could get good at them at the end," Pollack said.

The FLAW *is* the story at its essence. *Tootsie* is essentially about a man who <u>doesn't respect women</u>. Having Michael have to <u>pretend to be a woman</u> in the CATCH is a plot device to get him to face this FLAW, to begin to change, and to finally learn the opposite in the end in the STRENGTH of <u>respect for women</u>.

It may be a new concept to you to look for your protagonist's FLAW. We don't always think of a hero having a flaw. They're the hero! But no matter how noble your protagonist is, it is essential that you identify the FLAW that your CATCH is testing. No matter how much your protagonist may be a victim, you still must identify a FLAW in your protagonist that is at the crux of their story and that your protagonist will, in the end, overcome, change, and learn the opposite of in the STRENGTH (comedy), or fail to overcome, change, and learn the opposite of (tragedy).

A great example of giving a victim a real FLAW is the film *North Country*. This was a moving drama that, unfortunately, not many people saw. I'll describe it briefly, but if you have doubts that a victim can have a FLAW that is not only central to the story but also greatly increases our respect and understanding for the character, I urge you to see it yourself.

Josey Aimes (Charlize Theron) is leading a difficult life. Beaten by her husband, she escapes with her two kids to her parents' house. Her father asks if she cheated on her husband. Her mother urges her to reconcile. Josey can't seem to get respect from anyone in her small Minnesota town. She has a bad reputation stemming from her teen years, when she gave birth to her first child out of wedlock. When she refused to disclose the child's father, the assumption was she had had sex with so many different boys that she didn't know who the father was.

Throughout the story, Josey is a victim. When she hears the local mine has been legally forced to start hiring women and the wages are six times what she is making, she applies and is hired. But the women at the mine are unwanted, and they endure constant sexual harassment from the male miners: obscenities scrawled on their property, intimidating sexual threats, groping, and so on. She is targeted in particular by a supervisor who had briefly been a boyfriend of hers in high school, but things had ended badly. Finally she is physically and sexually attacked by this supervisor, and she quits. She convinces a lawyer to sue the mine for sexual harassment. On the stand, the mine's female lawyer brings up Josey's sexual history and suggests she doesn't know the identity of the father of her first child because she had numerous partners, including one of her high school teachers.

Now at this point in the film, I became very uncomfortable. Was the film suggesting that Josey's FLAW was "promiscuity" and that that was somehow the root of her problems? Because that is what everyone in the town seemed to think. But then, as part of her CLIMACTIC CHOICE to speak out, Josey feels forced to reveal her big secret: the father of her child is her high school teacher, who raped her, and her former boyfriend, now her supervisor, witnessed the attack and did nothing to help her.

The CLIMACTIC CHOICE is the first step a protagonist makes away from their FLAW and toward their STRENGTH in a comedy, and *North Country* is an Aristotelian comedy because Josey changes and learns in the end, and is therefore better off. I hadn't been able to determine the FLAW from Act 1 and Act 2, but now that I saw her CLIMACTIC CHOICE to speak out, and knowing that the CLIMACTIC CHOICE in a comedy is a step away from the FLAW and toward the STRENGTH, her FLAW finally dawned on me: she had a lack of self-worth. She felt so ashamed that she was raped and that her high school boyfriend didn't come to her aid that she felt she couldn't tell anyone about it. She'd been carrying this shame for years now even though keeping the rape a secret had only made her lack of self-worth grow. It led to the speculation that she wasn't revealing the identity of the father because she had so many partners. According to the defense, her "bad reputation" and supposed promiscuous ways contributed to this atmosphere of unchecked sexual harassment.

Is the screenwriter suggesting that Josey deserved what happened to her or is in some way responsible for the sexual harassment? No, absolutely not! No one deserves to be treated like that, no matter her reputation. She deserves justice in the courts, reputation or no reputation. But she also deserves to be free of the FLAW of feeling a <u>lack of self-worth</u> because of something someone else perpetrated.

And by feeling a <u>lack of self-worth</u> and keeping silent about the rape, she has contributed to her problems. Now, her FLAW of a <u>lack of self-worth</u> in no way exonerates the men of the mine or reduces their guilt one iota. But by letting her <u>lack of self-worth</u> keep her from reporting the rape, she allowed herself to be oppressed even more by men. She saw her rapist walk around free while she was further shamed with an uncalled-for bad reputation, and the bad reputation made her a greater target of sexual harassment. The men of the mine are no less guilty of sexual harassment than if none of this had happened, but she increased her own misery by letting the rape be a secret that oppressed her. By not reporting the rape, she gave her oppressors more power.

None of this reduces the guilt of the men of the mine in perpetrating an atmosphere of constant sexual harassment. In the real-life case the film *North Country* is based on, the women of the mine won their suit, the first class-action sexual harassment lawsuit in the US (it was overturned on appeal, but the mine settled with the women in the end). That's a fact.[2] But nobody wants to watch a protagonist who is only a victim, which is why the screenwriter probably added Josey's FLAW of <u>lack of self-worth</u> (the film *North Country* is considered a fictionalized account of this real-life case). As audiences, we want to see perpetrators get their comeuppance, but we need more than that. We also want to see protagonists with complete character arcs, and a complete character arc in a comedy requires that a character change 180 degrees from an initial FLAW to when in the end they learn the opposite, the STRENGTH. A comedy usually has a happy ending, and this is due not so much to happier circumstances in the plot but to the protagonist having learned the opposite of their FLAW and gained the STRENGTH, and therefore becoming a better, happier person.   [91]

Going through this horrible experience at the mine and finding that her FLAW of a <u>lack of self-worth</u> compounds her misery, Josey is finally pushed to change and make the CLIMACTIC CHOICE <u>to speak out</u> about the rape

Josey (Charlize Theron) completes her transformation from the FLAW of <u>lack of self-worth</u> to the STRENGTH of <u>pride</u> in her FINAL STEP in the last scene of the film. Still from *North Country*. Copyright 2005, Schematic Productions GmbH & Co. KG.

in her past, an action in the film that moves the other female workers at the mine to join her suit. In this CLIMACTIC CHOICE Josey is moving away from her FLAW of a <u>lack of self-worth</u> and toward the STRENGTH she will learn in the end: <u>pride</u>. When she speaks out about the rape, she isn't demonized. The defense attorney finally stops questioning her sexual history (in the real case all the women were questioned extensively in depositions about their sexual histories).[3] Josey learns that she has nothing to be ashamed of and that the abuse she has suffered at the hands of men has absolutely nothing to do with her and everything to do with the men. She should have <u>pride</u>, not shame, in her conduct. In the last scene, we see her take her FINAL STEP away from her FLAW of a <u>lack of self-worth</u> and toward the STRENGTH she ultimately gains, <u>pride</u>. She lets her eldest child take the wheel of her car for his first driving lesson, beaming with pride for him and for how she is raising him to be a good man.

Everyone has room to grow and change, and that is why your protagonist—no matter how noble they are, no matter how much a victim they are—should have a real FLAW to tackle at the center of their story, and, in a comedy, it should be one that will lead them to transform 180 degrees into someone who gains the opposite, the STRENGTH, in the end (in a tragedy, the protagonist fails to transform from their FLAW and fails to gain the opposite STRENGTH in the end).

If your character is truly a victim and bears no responsibility for their own misery, then they aren't the protagonist. In the film *The Accused* (not

Nutshelled), Jodie Foster won the Oscar for Best Actress in a Leading Role for her portrayal of Sarah Tobias, a woman gang-raped in a bar, but her character is not the protagonist (don't tell the Academy of Motion Picture Arts and Sciences). The deputy district attorney (played by Kelly McGillis) who prosecutes her attackers and the cheering bystanders is the protagonist, because she is the one who changes over the course of the story. Her FLAW is that she is judgmental, but by the end she has changed and learned the opposite, the STRENGTH of being empathetic.

Likewise in a tragedy, if a character commits a murder and gets away with it, they are not going to be the protagonist even if they are the character with the most screen time (see this exact example in the discussion of *Crimes and Misdemeanors* in Chapter 16, "Using a 'Secret Protagonist' to Structure a Nonconventional Story").

The overwhelming majority of feature films are Aristotelian comedies. In a comedy, the protagonist finds the ideal test of their FLAW in the CATCH, and this will lead them lower and lower. In Act 2 of a comedy, basically we the audience are laughing as bad things happen to the protagonist, taking them lower and lower. The protagonist reaches their lowest point, the CRISIS, at the end of Act 2. But at the CRISIS they will begin a transformation by making a CLIMACTIC CHOICE at the beginning of Act 3 that takes them away from their FLAW and toward the STRENGTH, and they will complete this transformation with the FINAL STEP. This transformation from their FLAW to what they learn, the STRENGTH, gives the protagonist in a comedy their usually happy ending.

In tragedies, protagonists also find themselves being tested in the CATCH by their FLAW, but from here until the end of the story they will have the opposite results from what they would have in a comedy. Throughout Act 2, the CATCH will test the FLAW, but in a tragedy the protagonist will usually come out on top of each test. This will take the tragic protagonist higher and higher until they reach their TRIUMPH, which is their highest moment of success in the story. At the CLIMACTIC CHOICE, instead of moving away from the FLAW, they will *fail to* change, and they will continue their flawed ways. At the FINAL STEP they will again fail an opportunity to change from their FLAW and thus will fail to gain the STRENGTH they needed to gain, and this will ultimately bring the protagonist their usually unhappy ending.

[93]

Let's look at this tragic progression in *Being John Malkovich*. Protagonist Craig Schwartz (John Cusack) gets his SET-UP WANT of <u>money</u> in the POINT OF NO RETURN when <u>he discovers a portal into</u> the soul of the famous actor <u>John Malkovich</u> (who is playing himself), and Craig <u>tells Maxine, who hatches a get-rich scheme</u> (23–30%: 0:26:42–0:34:25). The CATCH is his new business partner <u>Maxine is interested in only money and power</u>. This will become the perfect test of his FLAW: <u>pride</u>. Because of his <u>pride</u> and his obsession with Maxine, he tries to convince himself that Maxine really wants to be with him, when it is obvious to the audience that she is clearly only interested in the money and the power Craig gains when he becomes the famous actor John Malkovich.

His ultimate TRIUMPH, which is both the point of his highest success and the ultimate manifestation of his SET-UP WANT for <u>money</u>, is at 1:28:06–1:28:33 (78%): <u>as John Malkovich, he has everything: fame, riches, and Maxine</u>. He makes the wrong CLIMACTIC CHOICE, one that furthers his FLAW of <u>pride</u>, when Maxine is kidnapped. Lester says they will kill her if Craig doesn't leave Malkovich, so <u>he abandons Malkovich, hoping this will prove his love to Maxine</u>. But Maxine wants nothing to do with the real Craig Schwartz, and she reconciles with Lotte. Craig further compounds his misery in his FINAL STEP when inside their seven-year-old child's soul, he tries, unsuccessfully, to get the child's eyes to move away but <u>he can't avoid the sight of Maxine and Lotte embracing</u>. He has a tragic ending because he failed to learn the STRENGTH of <u>humility</u>.

Learning or experiencing humility in the very end is too late for a comedic ending. In a comedy, the protagonist moves away from their FLAW and toward the STRENGTH in both their CLIMACTIC CHOICE and their FINAL STEP. *Being John Malkovich* is a tragedy because Craig furthered his FLAW of <u>pride</u>, instead of moving away from it, when in the CLIMACTIC CHOICE he entertained the notion that Maxine might be moved enough by his sacrifice to love him in return, even though he had just protested to Lester that he'd be nothing to Maxine if he left Malkovich. The FINAL STEP further continues his FLAW of <u>pride</u> when he tries and fails to control the child's eyes.

When applying the Nutshell Technique to your own stories, you want to try and write as few words on the Nutshell Technique form as possible, and the FLAW is definitely an item that can often be summed up in one

[94]

word. You want to also try to state your protagonist's FLAW in universal terms (e.g., "greed") and try not to get into plot in your FLAW description (e.g., "wants inheritance now"). Think Seven Deadly Sins-type FLAWs. Here's my mnemonic for the Seven Deadly Sins, PEG'S LAW:

Pride
Envy
Gluttony
Sloth
Lust
Avarice (which means greed, but you need the "A" for the mnemonic)
Wrath

You want your protagonist's FLAW to sound as flawed as possible. "Pride" can be a good thing, so make sure that if you use it as a FLAW that it is in a negative sense, such as the undue <u>pride</u> Craig has in *Being John Malkovich*. Ideally your FLAW is something your audience would react negatively toward. Josey's FLAW of <u>lack of self-worth</u> in *North Country* isn't the most egregious FLAW I've ever heard, but in the context of the film, it works because it is the piece of her misery for which she is responsible and from which she needs to change to learn the opposite in the STRENGTH.

Generally you want your FLAW to sound as unsympathetic as possible. Here are some word choices that demonstrate this. These more nuanced word choices for your protagonist's FLAW add specificity to your character and heighten the emotional journey when they are tested by the CATCH.

Instead of:	*Try:*
pride	egotism, arrogance, or hubris
sheepishness	passivity
shyness	inferiority complex
idealism	naiveté or ignorance
daring	recklessness
single-mindedness	myopia or obsession
certainty	self-righteousness
lack of confidence	loss of faith in self

[95]

Make sure that the FLAW is something that is truly your protagonist's fault, something they have control over and thus can change (or fail to change, in the case of a tragedy). In *The Bourne Identity*, Jason Bourne has amnesia, which he can't help and has no control over, so it's not the FLAW. In Act 2, he begins to piece together his past, and toward the end of Act 2, he arrives at the full truth about his identity: he's a CIA-contracted assassin, and now he's considered a rogue whom the CIA wants to destroy. This also isn't his FLAW, because he can't control the past. What he can control is how he behaves in the present, and every time he encounters an authority figure or one of the assassins after him, he immediately reacts with deadly force. His FLAW is he reacts unconsciously. He behaves as though he's still a CIA assassin, an identity that he begins to realize he wants nothing to do with. So in Act 3 he begins to change, and by the end he has learned the opposite, the STRENGTH to live life consciously.

Something like "mental illness" wouldn't be a FLAW because the protagonist must have the ability to change the FLAW and learn the opposite. "Alcoholic" isn't really a FLAW in the sense we are looking for. Alcoholism is better categorized (for our purposes) as external behavior and as an effect of some other underlying internal FLAW. The question the writer needs to ask is: what is the root FLAW of the character that led to this alcoholism? The answer is going to be different for different alcoholics. Is the root FLAW "selfishness"? Someone who is an alcoholic is ultimately being selfish, certainly, if they have any family or anyone else living with them. "My enjoyment of alcohol is more important than you," the alcoholic is ultimately saying by not giving it up. So for one alcoholic protagonist, the FLAW might be best described as "selfishness." But for another alcoholic, perhaps one who lives alone, the central FLAW might be better summed up as "lack of self-worth." In the past, the alcoholism and the protagonist's selfishness in not giving it up drove the protagonist's wife to leave him. Now, as this particular screenplay begins, he's a miserable alcoholic divorcé who is well aware he has a problem with alcohol. It's so bad a problem, in fact, that he feels no one would want to live with him or love him. His central FLAW at this point isn't "alcoholic" or "selfish" but "lack of self-worth."

[96]

You also want to make sure you identify just one central FLAW and corresponding STRENGTH for your protagonist. Your protagonist has multiple flaws, just like all of us in life have more than one flaw (I'm sorry to tell you). But you want to identify no more than one FLAW and STRENGTH on the Nutshell Technique form. There needs to be only one central FLAW that your protagonist is going to change from and learn in the STRENGTH, its opposite, in the end, in a comedy (in a tragedy, the protagonist will fail to learn the STRENGTH). Having two or more Nutshell FLAWs and STRENGTHs doesn't fortify your story; it dilutes it.

That was the problem with the film *Argo,* which may have won the Academy Award for Best Picture but failed to fully engage me. Protagonist Tony Mendez lacked a strong central FLAW, and so the STRENGTH he gains didn't feel connected to his journey. A couple of FLAWs are hinted at: values job over family, "loner," and "feels overly responsible." *Argo* is an Aristotelian comedy because the protagonist changes and is better off in the end. But in a comedy, we should see the protagonist move away from the FLAW and toward the STRENGTH in the CLIMACTIC CHOICE, and we didn't see this in *Argo*. After his CRISIS when his boss tells him the mission (to sneak six American embassy employees out of Iran) is off (64–65%: 1:16:44–1:17:43), his CLIMACTIC CHOICE is he tells his boss he's responsible for them and he's defying orders. This CLIMACTIC CHOICE isn't doing anything to move Tony away from any of his three possible FLAWs (values job over family, "loner," and "feels overly responsible"). In fact, this CLIMACTIC CHOICE reflects an increase of all three FLAWs in Tony (he's valuing job over family, he's making a loner decision, and he feels overly responsible).

In the FINAL STEP, he reunites with his family. He arrives at his wife's door and then watches his son fall asleep. It is implied that he has learned the STRENGTH values family, although I wouldn't go as far to say that he has learned he "values family over job," which would be the true opposite of the FLAW of values job over family. It is also unclear how or why this journey rescuing the six Americans caused him to gain this STRENGTH. If he truly had learned that he "values family over job" from this journey, we would have seen him make a CLIMACTIC CHOICE that involved him choosing his family over the mission, such as if he abandoned the mission for his family. Obviously that wouldn't work since it doesn't reflect the actual historical events and would give the mission a negative outcome. But by not having the CLIMACTIC CHOICE show a change in the protago-

[97]

nist away from the FLAW of <u>values job over family</u> toward the STRENGTH of <u>values family</u>, the STRENGTH seems to come out of nowhere in the FINAL STEP.

And in Act 3, he doesn't move away from the other two FLAWs: "loner" and "feels overly responsible." I imagine that on his next mission he will be just as much a loner and will feel just as overly responsible as he did during the Argo mission. He didn't learn their opposites: the STRENGTHs of "values community" and "able to let go."

His CLIMACTIC CHOICE when <u>he tells his boss he's responsible for them and he's defying orders</u> reflects someone learning the STRENGTH of being a "maverick." This would have made a much stronger STRENGTH than <u>values family</u>, which was what the film suggests he gained, because it is unclear how he learned to value family from this mission. But for "maverick" to work as a STRENGTH in the end, we would need to see him have the opposite trait as a FLAW in Acts 1 and 2: "by the book." And Tony doesn't have this FLAW. If he had had the FLAW of being "by the book" in Act 1 and 2, seeing him become a "maverick" in Act 3 would have made for a much more fitting STRENGTH to gain than <u>values family</u>.

Another direction we could go to tweak Tony's FLAW-to-STRENGTH character arc and improve the story would be to have him go from the FLAW of "loner" to a STRENGTH of "values community." I'm encouraged by the moment in the existing film at the airport where the one embassy employee who speaks Farsi steps up to explain to the Iranian customs officials what the storyboards depict. It's a brief moment where someone other than Tony takes the lead. It doesn't go so far as to show Tony moving to the STRENGTH of "values community," but the plot could have been tweaked so that it did. It would have required having Tony really stick to his flawed "loner" ways in Act 2, perhaps going so far as to specifically demand that all six Americans never, ever take the lead and always do the plan exactly as he's laid it out. And it would mean changing the CLIMACTIC CHOICE from what it is in the film (<u>he tells his boss he's responsible for them and he's defying orders</u>) to a CLIMACTIC CHOICE that exemplifies Tony moving away from "loner" and toward the STRENGTH of "values community."

[98]

For changing Tony's CLIMACTIC CHOICE, I'm inspired by the FLAW-to-STRENGTH character arc in *Witness*, because John Book's FLAW is that he's

John Book (Harrison Ford) begins his transformation from his FLAW of <u>loner</u> to its opposite, the STRENGTH of <u>values community</u>, in his CLIMACTIC CHOICE <u>to face [his enemy] the Amish way, as a group all bearing witness</u>. Still from *Witness*. Copyright 1985, Paramount Pictures Corporation.

a <u>loner</u> and he learns the STRENGTH that he <u>values community</u>. In the CLIMACTIC CHOICE, Book is confronted by his former boss who has come to kill him, and the Amish men and women come forward and rally around him. His CLIMACTIC CHOICE is <u>to face him the Amish way, as a group all bearing witness</u>. A dozen unarmed Amish have a standoff with one man with a gun, who sees he can't win and puts down his weapon.

To show Tony's FLAW-to-STRENGTH arc from "loner" to "values community" in *Argo*, the CLIMACTIC CHOICE could have been "the six embassy employees insist that with Tony they are a community of seven and they must all go through despite Tony's orders" instead of it just being Tony's CLIMACTIC CHOICE of <u>defying orders</u>. This would have required changing the nature of the characters of the six embassy employees, who in the existing film are portrayed as being somewhat cowardly and having limited confidence in the mission's success. But it would have made for a more interesting change and ultimate STRENGTH for Tony to learn he "values community" in the end. The obstacles at the airport could have all [99] been moments where, instead of Tony taking the lead, Tony and the embassy employees are required to rely on and trust one another in this community of seven if they are going to make it on the plane.

If you are concerned that we're taking too many liberties with *Argo*, since it was based on historical events, you shouldn't be. Tweaking Tony's FLAW to "by the book" or his STRENGTH to "values community" would require relatively minor changes to the story compared to the actual changes from real-life events the filmmakers made in the existing film. Either tweak would have made for a more satisfying character arc for the protagonist and would have shown a real change in the protagonist that was directly connected to his journey of having gone through the Argo mission.

One final caveat: watch out that your FLAW and your SET-UP WANT aren't related. For example, if the protagonist's FLAW is "greed," don't have a SET-UP WANT of "money." Your story becomes too one-dimensional and too obviously a morality tale. Let the FLAW be tested by the CATCH, not the SET-UP WANT.

The FLAW and how your protagonist deals with it are what your story is secretly about. Finding the precise word (or words) expressing the FLAW and establishing its polar opposite in the STRENGTH will bring focus and clarity to your story.

Chapter

10

CRISIS

If a story is a comedy, the protagonist will reach their **CRISIS**, *which:*

- occurs near the 75% mark (around page 90 in a 120-page script or 1:30:00 in a two-hour film)
- is the protagonist's lowest point
- is the exact opposite state of mind or situation from where the protagonist was in the SET-UP WANT

Also:

- it puts the protagonist between two bad choices, a rock and a hard place, with no solution in sight
- it is right before the protagonist makes a CLIMACTIC CHOICE away from the FLAW and toward the STRENGTH

Film Nutshells Discussed in This Chapter

Braveheart
The Bourne Identity

Collateral

Casablanca

Titanic

Pulp Fiction

The Godfather

Witness

Tootsie

Dallas Buyers Club

ACT 2 COMES TO AN END by about the 75% point in a film or screenplay, which is 1:30:00 in a two-hour film or page 90 of a 120-page screenplay. It is here that the protagonist will reach their lowest point in an Aristotelian comedy; screenwriters refer to this moment by terms such as Plot Point 2, the Break into Act 3, the Second Reversal, or the term I use, the CRISIS. In a tragedy, the protagonist will instead reach their highest point at this 75% mark, and this I call their TRIUMPH. Let the alliteration of comedy/CRISIS and tragedy/TRIUMPH help you to remember the two distinct directions a story takes depending on whether it is a comedy or tragedy.

How do you determine whether a story is an Aristotelian comedy or a tragedy? Usually a "happy ending" or "sad ending" is the tip-off, but not always. In a tragedy the protagonist experiences a change of fortune in Act 3 from good to bad due in part to their own internal FLAW. In the end they are usually worse off; that is, they have a sad ending. An Aristotelian comedy is essentially the opposite. The comedic protagonist experiences a change of fortune in Act 3 from bad to good due to their ability to overcome their FLAW and learn its opposite, the STRENGTH. In the end, they are usually better off; that is, they have a happy ending (see the discussion of Aristotle and the origin of the definitions of comedy and tragedy in Chapter 1 notes).

To determine whether a story is an Aristotelian comedy or a tragedy, you need to look at the protagonist's central FLAW and whether in the end they learn the opposite and gain the STRENGTH (comedy) or not (tragedy). *Braveheart*, believe it or not, is a comedy. It is not common for a comedy to show a protagonist being eviscerated and killed, but *Braveheart* is such a case. William Wallace gains the STRENGTH of supreme courage so that he can withstand torture. He refuses to swear allegiance and consciously chooses this path, knowing his courage will be an inspiration for genera-tions of Scots after him. To him, it is a happy ending.

Probably 95% of feature films are Aristotelian comedies. I'm going to ad-dress comedies and their protagonists' CRISIS first, and in the next chap-ter I'll address tragedies and their protagonists' TRIUMPH.

By the end of Act 1, the screenwriter has given the protagonist their SET-UP WANT in the POINT OF NO RETURN. As the protagonist begins Act 2, a major conflict has been removed from the story—wanting the WANT—but the screenwriter has also given the protagonist the CATCH, which is a new problem and an ideal test of the protagonist's FLAW, and this restores conflict. This is a must-have, because once there is no conflict, the story is essentially over. The CATCH is a new problem for the protago-nist, but one they believe they can handle. So in Act 2 as the protagonist goes about trying to best the CATCH, it's the screenwriter's job to throw obstacle after obstacle in their way. In Act 2 of a comedy, we the audience are essentially watching bad things happen to the protagonist as we laugh at them (or sympathize with them), and things get worse and worse. These obstacles are going to take the protagonist lower and lower until they hit rock bottom at the CRISIS.

Take care that the CRISIS isn't brought on by bad fortune or some exter-nal tragic event over which the protagonist has no control. Although they may have had some bad luck here and there, the CRISIS should be a prod-uct at least partially of the protagonist's creation. Their own FLAW should be a big part of what brings them to their own personal hell in the CRISIS.

The CRISIS has two requirements. The first is that it's the protagonist's absolute lowest point in the story. They should be stuck between a rock and hard place, in their own personal hell. The second is that the protago-nist should be in the exact opposite state of mind or situation from where they were in the SET-UP WANT. Often I see screenwriters fail to meet one or both of these requirements, but it's important to achieve both.

The lower the CRISIS takes the protagonist, the greater emotional dis-tance they will be from the equilibrium they were in at the beginning of the story. And the greater the emotional distance means the more pro-found the change and transformation will be. In a comedy, the protago-nist will make a 180-degree change from their FLAW to its polar opposite, the STRENGTH, by the very end. In order to achieve this about-face, the writer needs to take their protagonist to the protagonist's own rock bottom, where no good options are in sight. Only at this lowest point with no good options will the protagonist be forced to finally change and move in a direction different from their FLAW.

Bringing the protagonist in the CRISIS to the opposite state of mind or situation from where they were in the SET-UP WANT is another measure of just how much the protagonist has changed from who they were in the beginning. And it brings this change to light with delicious irony: what they once so wanted, they now hate.

In the beginning of *The Bourne Identity*, protagonist Jason Bourne has been rescued by a fishing boat and has no memory of his past. In his first dialogue scene a fisherman asks him, "What's your name?" He replies, "I don't know." His SET-UP WANT is to figure out who he is. In the POINT OF NO RETURN a safe-deposit box reveals he's Jason Bourne and has multiple passports, a gun, and cash. From that point on, he is on the run from the authorities and from assassins sent by the CIA to destroy him. At 1:13:26 he finally learns the full extent of his past: he was an assassin, and having no memory of this and no connection to this part of his identity, he's horrified by this knowledge. He and his love interest, Marie, hide out at the house of a family Marie knows. His CRISIS is at 1:23:06–1:23:17 (70% into the running time), when in the middle of the night, he can't sleep, and he goes to check on the children sleeping in the house. Not only are his and Marie's lives in danger, but now he's endangered the lives of this family. He tells Marie: "I don't want to know who I am anymore. . . . Everything I found out, I wanna forget."

I love to point to *The Bourne Identity*'s SET-UP WANT/CRISIS opposition. His WANT was to figure out who he is; at the CRISIS he says, "I don't want to know who I am anymore." Exact opposites. Too often screenwriters fail to bring their protagonists to the opposite state of mind or opposite situation in the CRISIS. In failing to do so, they are missing a great opportunity to show their protagonist go through a profound reversal.

Having a SET-UP WANT and a CRISIS that are truly opposites can make or break a screenplay. See the chart on the next page for a number of protagonists' SET-UP WANTs and their wonderfully ironic corresponding CRISES.

Casablanca is a great film specifically, I think, because of the opposition of the protagonist's SET-UP WANT and his CRISIS. Rick's WANT is to stick his "neck out for nobody." At the CRISIS, he has won back his lover,

[104]

Aristotelian Comedies: Set-Up Wants and Their Corresponding Crises

FILM	SET-UP WANT	CRISIS
Collateral	For the passenger to not want to leave his car	He wants him *out* of the car (and flips it over to get him out)
Casablanca	To stick his "neck out for nobody"	He has to stick his neck out for everybody: the fate of the world is in his hands
Braveheart	A reason to fight	Unable to fight: he's been betrayed, and he collapses and has to be carried off the field
Titanic	To go overboard	Doesn't want to be overboard
Pulp Fiction	To prevent Marsellus from being "fucked like a bitch"	Marsellus is "fucked like a bitch," literally, when he is raped by Zed
The Godfather	To stay out of the family business	Don Corleone says that Michael is now the head of the family
Witness	To find the killer	The killer finds him
Blade Runner (not Nutshelled)	To kill replicants	Replicant is going to kill him
Casino Royale (not Nutshelled)	To kill his enemy	To save his enemy (Vesper is the enemy and is drowning)
Jaws (not Nutshelled)	To protect his son from danger	His own son is attacked by the shark

Ilsa, and she is eager to leave her husband, Victor Laszlo, and escape Casablanca with Rick, using his two letters of transit for safe passage. But if she leaves with Rick, Laszlo will be trapped in Casablanca, where he surely will be imprisoned by the Nazis. And Laszlo may be one of the Allies' best hopes to win the war. As keenly observed by the Nazi Major Strasser, unlike other Resistance leaders, Laszlo could never be replaced, and these French provinces of Africa are just waiting for a leader like Laszlo. So what is the CRISIS for Rick, the man whose SET-UP WANT is <u>to stick his "neck out for nobody"</u>? His CRISIS is <u>he has to stick his neck out for everybody: the fate of the world is in his hands</u>.

[105]

Today's audiences often miss this point: the irony of a man who doesn't want to stick his neck out for anybody having to stick it out for everybody. It requires paying attention to a lot of exposition to put together that if Ilsa leaves Laszlo, Laszlo is likely doomed because of the Nazis, and without Laszlo, the Allies could lose. It's also easy to miss the CRISIS and its irony because it essentially happens off screen. We never see or hear Rick express his CRISIS, that <u>he has to stick his neck out for everybody: the fate of the world is in his hands</u>. The closest there is to the CRISIS being on screen is when Ilsa wonders what will happen to Laszlo when they leave and says she doesn't know what is right anymore at 1:25:03–1:25:19 (82%). "You have to think for both us, for all of us," she tells Rick. "All right, I will," he replies.

I think *Casablanca* could have benefited from having had such an on-screen lament. It's an extremely important moment, but since the CRISIS that <u>he has to stick his neck out for everybody: the fate of the world is in his hands</u> happens essentially off screen, it's easy to miss. How could the film-makers have shown it on screen? A poor choice would have been to have Rick alone talk to himself about the dilemma, because in life people do talk to themselves, but they tend to mutter and not speak in well-thought-out sentences. Another poor choice would be to hear Rick's thoughts in a voiceover, but you don't want to use voiceover on only one occasion, and to add Rick's voiceover throughout would have been heavy-handed. I think that a moment to explicitly show his CRISIS on screen would have been best handled in dialogue. I understand that he wouldn't have wanted Ilsa to know his dilemma and his doubts, but he could have confided in Sam, his piano player, much like earlier when he drunkenly bemoans to Sam all the pain he is in from Ilsa walking into his bar. I like that Rick usually keeps his feelings bottled up, but the film could have benefited from another moment when he lets them out, especially since without this scene, some viewers miss the CRISIS and its profound irony altogether.

For your CRISIS to work, it needs to be more than just something vaguely negative for the protagonist. Try to find a CRISIS that is not only your protagonist's lowest point but also puts your protagonist in the exact opposite state of mind or situation from where they were at their SET-UP WANT. Ideally at the CRISIS they will hate what they most wanted at the SET-UP WANT. And don't assume that your audience will figure out that your protagonist must be in the opposite state of mind. The audience can't know your protagonist's thoughts unless you use voiceover. So at the CRISIS, have your protagonist do something that explicitly demonstrates that they want the opposite of their SET-UP WANT, or have them say it, like Jason Bourne did.

A less common problem with the CRISIS is that it fails to meet the first requirement: it is the protagonist's lowest point in the story. In *Tootsie*, Michael Dorsey's CRISIS is when his love interest, Julie, <u>says she can't be friends anymore, and he wants *out* of the job</u> (86–87%: 1:40:08–1:41:17). He's in an ironclad contract and has to be on the soap for another year. This CRISIS would never fly had it been presented in one of my workshops, I joke with my writers, because it fails the first requirement of the CRISIS: it's not low enough. He wants out of a high-paying soap opera job? That's the lowest the screenwriter can take him? What if he wanted out of a high-paying job *and* he was in jail? How about if he was considering suicide? In many Frank Capra films, the protagonist is considering suicide at the CRISIS, since that's pretty much as low as you can go. I suppose suicide doesn't fit with the tone of *Tootsie*, but you get the idea. You need to think almost like a sadist to find your protagonist's own personal hell in their CRISIS.

The second requirement for the CRISIS, which *Tootsie* passes with flying colors, is that the protagonist is at the exact opposite state of mind as he was at the SET-UP WANT. What was Michael's SET-UP WANT? A <u>job</u>. What is his CRISIS? He <u>wants *out* of the job</u>, the exact opposite of his first-scene WANT.

A really good CRISIS in a film should be an "Ah-ha!" moment for the viewer who is studying the Nutshell Technique. It's a clever, ironic twist, and irony is a writer's best friend. The protagonist has shifted 180 degrees and now wants the exact opposite of what they wanted in their first scene.

One caveat: sometimes I see writers inadvertently state a CRISIS that, instead of being the opposite of the SET-UP WANT, is actually a repeat of the SET-UP WANT. Let's say you had a protagonist who WANTs "money." In the POINT OF NO RETURN "a job is offered to them" and therefore they get their WANT of "money." Over Act 2, they grow to hate the job, and by the CRISIS "they hate the job so much they quit." But "they hate the job so much they quit" isn't the opposite of the WANT of "money"; it's actually

[107]

the same thing. Because what do they want now that they quit their job? Money. So you end up with a SET-UP WANT of "money" and the CRISIS is "they hate the job so much they quit, and now they want money." So make sure that over the course of Act 2 the protagonist truly moves to the opposite state of mind about the thing they initially wanted in the SET-UP WANT.

Alternatively, you could make it pointless at the time of the CRISIS for the protagonist to want the WANT. *Casablanca* works this way. Rick can continue to wish he didn't have to stick his neck out for anybody but it doesn't matter. The fate of world is in his hands because he holds the letters of transit. No matter what decision he makes about who gets them, he's sticking his neck out. Use the letters himself, and then he's responsible for the possibility of the Allies losing. Give the letters to Laszlo and Ilsa, and then he's risking his own life.

The Shawshank Redemption (not Nutshelled) works similarly. Protagonist Andy Dufresne's (Tim Robbins) SET-UP WANT is: for everybody to know he's innocent. Late in Act 2, a new inmate, Tommy, realizes that a former cellmate of his had bragged about committing the double murder for which Andy was convicted. Andy tells the warden, but the warden doesn't want Andy freed, and the CRISIS is: Tommy is murdered by the warden, and now no one will ever know Andy's innocent. Tommy was Andy's only chance to have his conviction overturned. It is pointless for Andy to continue to WANT for everybody to know he's innocent. He has lost all hope of proving his innocence and no longer wants or pursues it.

The CRISIS typically puts the protagonist in between two bad options, a rock and a hard place, and the audience should feel that there is no other way out of this dilemma. At Andy's CRISIS his two bad options are: abandon all hope and accept that he will die behind bars for a crime he did not commit, or commit suicide (he asks Red to procure rope, and Red is certain he will use it to hang himself). At Rick's CRISIS, his two bad options are: escape with the love of his life but be responsible for the possibility of the Allies losing World War II, or lose the love of his life a second time and be trapped in Casablanca.

[108]

Make sure that in your CRISIS your protagonist is also between a rock and a hard place. Sometimes I see screenwriters put their protagonist between a rock and a soft place; for example, the protagonist could stay with her husband in a miserable marriage or leave with her lover and run away to Europe. That's not going to work. You need to find two bad options so there is a sense of no way out.

Here's how I Nutshell films I see in the movie theater. Instead of guessing at the SET-UP WANT, I scribble down a description of what is happening and bits of key dialogue in the first few dialogue scenes. The POINT OF NO RETURN is relatively easy to identify because it tends to occur around twenty to thirty minutes into the film, it happens *to* the protagonist, and it's a turning point that makes this movie *this* movie. At the POINT OF NO RETURN I reflect back on the first dialogue scenes I scribbled down and consider what possible SET-UP WANT(s) the protagonist got in it. Sometimes I see a possible SET-UP WANT and sometimes I don't, but I definitely don't know I have the correct SET-UP WANT until I get to the CRISIS or TRIUMPH at around 1:30:00. Here it should be apparent whether the protagonist is at their lowest point, which would mean that it is a comedy and they reached their CRISIS, or their highest point, which would mean it is a tragedy and they reached their TRIUMPH. And now is the first time I can know if I have the correct SET-UP WANT. I consider whether at the CRISIS the protagonist has reached the opposite state of mind or situation from what I theorized the SET-UP WANT to be (comedy), or whether at the TRIUMPH they have reached the ultimate manifestation of my theoretical SET-UP WANT (tragedy).

If my guess for the SET-UP WANT turns out to be incorrect, or if I didn't have a guess, now at the CRISIS/TRIUMPH I can try to reverse-engineer and use the CRISIS/TRIUMPH to determine the SET-UP WANT. If it's a comedy and the protagonist reaches a CRISIS, they should now be at the opposite state of mind or situation that they were in at their SET-UP WANT. If it's a tragedy and the protagonist reaches their TRIUMPH, the TRIUMPH should be the ultimate manifestation of the SET-UP WANT. But I also need to consider whether, in both comedies and tragedies, the protagonist got this SET-UP WANT in the POINT OF NO RETURN, because that is another requirement of the Nutshell Technique.

I saw *Dallas Buyers Club* in the theater, and here is how I Nutshelled [109] it as I watched it. In the first scene of the movie, protagonist Ron Woodroof (Matthew McConaughey) is having sex with a woman and snorting cocaine in a bull stall as he watches a cowboy ride a bull out in front of a rodeo audience. A second woman is revealed in the stall, and he switches to having sex with her. I scribbled down (yes, I bring a notebook to movies), "sex and drugs with two women at rodeo."

At 0:08:18, Ron winds up in the hospital, where he is told a blood test was administered, he tested positive for HIV, and he only has a month to live. I knew that this moment was not the POINT OF NO RETURN but instead what it is often confused with: the Inciting Incident. This is because (1) it happens too early in the 117-minute running time, and (2) it doesn't change everything and put us past a "point of no return." It's 1985 at this point in the film, and at that time, AIDS was seen as a "gay illness," and Ron, an avowed heterosexual in the film, is in complete disbelief and is convinced the hospital mixed up his blood test with somebody else's.

At 0:17:40, Ron is at the library, looking at newspaper articles about AIDS. He focuses in on a phrase, "intravenous drug users," and then on another one, "unprotected sex." Then the film goes into a flashback as Ron remembers something. We see him having sex with a woman. He looks at a snake tattoo on her back that goes up to her neck and down to her arm—which is riddled with track marks. The film cuts back to the library, where Ron pounds the desk in anger. Now we're at a POINT OF NO RETURN: the newspaper articles make him realize that he contracted HIV from promiscuous unprotected sex, and he finally accepts that he is HIV positive. Now his world has completely changed, and he is past a POINT OF NO RETURN.

I'm going to hold off on determining the exact wording of the POINT OF NO RETURN, but it has to do with the newspaper articles and his acceptance of the diagnosis. My hunch of the SET-UP WANT that he got in the POINT OF NO RETURN is promiscuous sex. He wants promiscuous sex when he is having sex with two different women in the first scene. His adult life has been filled with promiscuous sex. And now at the POINT OF NO RETURN it dawns on him what the awful CATCH is for him from having had all this promiscuous sex: he realizes promiscuous sex led to him being HIV positive.

At this point in the film, I am guessing as to Ron's SET-UP WANT of promiscuous sex. It's the only thing I can think of that he wanted in the first scene that he gets in the POINT OF NO RETURN. But I could be wrong. Because whatever the SET-UP WANT is in the first scene, at the end of Act 2 the protagonist must either experience the opposite of the SET-UP WANT

[110]

in the CRISIS, in the case of a comedy, or the ultimate manifestation of the SET-UP WANT in the TRIUMPH, in the case of a tragedy.

I knew a little about *Dallas Buyers Club* and the real-life story it was based on before I saw it. I knew that Ron died in the end, but I also suspected it would be an Aristotelian comedy because I had read descriptions of the film that suggested Ron was an unpleasant, homophobic man who changed after he started the buyers club. So I thought that despite his inevitable death, it would be a happy ending for audiences because we would see him become a better person and also see him live a lot longer than the month the doctor initially gave him.

If *Dallas Buyers Club* is an Aristotelian comedy, this means things are going to get worse and worse for the protagonist in Act 2 until the end of Act 2, when the protagonist reaches their lowest point, their CRISIS. In Act 2, Ron is facing an uphill battle. In 1985 there were no approved drugs for the treatment of HIV. He quickly realizes he can get unapproved drugs and other supplements to treat HIV in Mexico, and also that he will make a lot of money if he smuggles these drugs and supplements to other HIV patients in the US. It's illegal to sell these, but it's not illegal to sell memberships to a buyers club that gives the medications away to members for free, thus the Dallas Buyers Club. He partners with Rayon, who is HIV positive and transgendered, so that he can approach the gay HIV-positive community with his club. The venture is constantly challenged by government agencies and fined, and at one point the law is changed, making buyer clubs illegal. He continues to run it and now gives away the drugs, although this obviously can't last. His club is now illegal and unsustainable. Initially homophobic, he grows emotionally close to Rayon over these ordeals. He seems to reach his lowest point when Rayon dies from AIDS-related complications. But this isn't the opposite of the SET-UP WANT that I suspected, promiscuous sex. I had a hunch he was going to feel even lower. He makes a scene at the hospital, calling a doctor he is at odds with a murderer, and has to be removed by security. Then he goes to a motel with a hooker. The hooker strips and then unbuckles his pants to give him oral sex. Suddenly, Ron stops her, pushes her away from him, and breaks down and cries. For the first time, he turns down sex, which is the opposite of the state of mind he had in the SET-UP WANT (promiscuous sex). Here's how I phrased the CRISIS, at 1:34:50–1:36:50 (80–83%): Rayon dies, and for the first time Ron

[111]

turns down sex. Now at the CRISIS I can confirm that my guess of its oppo-site, promiscuous sex, was the correct SET-UP WANT.

Hopefully you've heeded my advice and held off in determining your protagonist's SET-UP WANT. When you consider your CRISIS, it's a good time to begin thinking about the SET-UP WANT.

For the CRISIS, think of as many miserable things as you can that your protagonist could go through toward the end of Act 2. Remember: you want to think almost like a sadist and take your protagonist as low as pos-sible. Then consider if any of these misfortunes have opposites that could be your protagonist's SET-UP WANT in the beginning of your story.

As an example, let's suppose in the CRISIS your protagonist "has been exposed in a very embarrassing public scandal and their photo is plas-tered on the covers of tabloid magazines." One possible SET-UP WANT that would work in opposition to this CRISIS is: "to be famous." Your protago-nist would need to begin the story as someone who wasn't in the public eye but craved fame; their SET-UP WANT is "to be famous." In the POINT OF NO RETURN, they would become famous somehow and thus get their WANT "to be famous." In Act 2, your protagonist would begin to discover, as you, the writer, throw obstacle after obstacle in their way, that fame isn't all it's cracked up to be. At the CRISIS your protagonist "has been exposed in a very embarrassing public scandal and their photo is plastered on the covers of tabloid magazines"—and we'll add this to the CRISIS statement to make it abundantly clear that the protagonist has reached the opposite state of mind from where they were in their SET-UP WANT—"and they wish they had never become famous."

The CRISIS needs to fulfill two important criteria. Make sure that you maximize your protagonist's emotional journey by creating a CRISIS that is the absolute lowest you can take them. And don't forgo the opportunity to show the delicious irony of your protagonist hating what they once so coveted by bringing them to a CRISIS that is the opposite of their SET-UP

WANT.

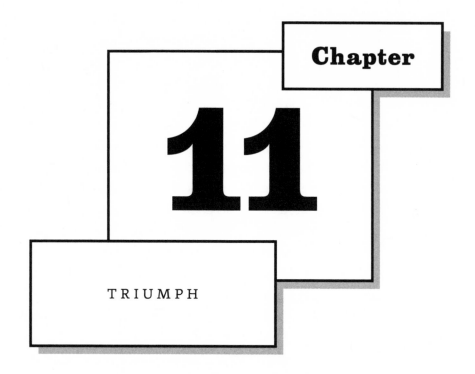

Chapter

11

TRIUMPH

If a story is a tragedy, the protagonist will reach their **TRIUMPH**, which:

- occurs near the 75% mark (page 90 in a 120-page script or 1:30:00 in a two-hour film)
- is the protagonist's highest point
- is the ultimate manifestation of the protagonist's SET-UP WANT

Also:

- it typically puts the protagonist between two good options
- it is right before the protagonist makes a CLIMACTIC CHOICE in which they fail an opportunity to move away from the FLAW and toward the STRENGTH

Film Nutshells Discussed in This Chapter

Sunset Blvd.
Chinatown
Annie Hall

The Usual Suspects
Being John Malkovich
Memento
The Social Network

IF A STORY IS A TRAGEDY, the protagonist will reach not their CRISIS but instead their TRIUMPH at around the 75% point, which is 1:30:00 in a two-hour film or page 90 of a 120-page screenplay. The TRIUMPH has two requirements. The first is that it's the protagonist's absolute highest point in the story. Throughout Act 2, the screenwriter has thrown obstacle after obstacle in the protagonist's way, just like in a comedy. But unlike in a comedy, the tragic protagonist will come out mainly on top after each obstacle, and their fortune will rise and rise until they reach their pinnacle of success at the very end of Act 2 in the TRIUMPH.

The second requirement of the TRIUMPH is that, instead of reaching the opposite state of mind or situation from their SET-UP WANT, as they would in a comedy, in a tragedy the protagonist will experience the ultimate manifestation of their initial SET-UP WANT.

Let's look at the tragic progression in *Sunset Blvd.*, perhaps still the greatest film Hollywood has ever made about itself. Protagonist Joe Gillis's SET-UP WANT is a writing job. He's an out-of-work screenwriter, and he's flat broke. Repo men have come for his car. Joe manages to give them the slip, but not before his car blows a tire in front of an old Hollywood mansion, and he meets the mansion's owner, Norma Desmond, a former silent film star. The POINT OF NO RETURN is a former silent film star hires him to rewrite a script for her comeback (21–22%: 0:23:07–0:23:57). So he achieves his SET-UP WANT of a writing job, but the CATCH is the script is terrible, and she's delusional. That's the perfect test of his FLAW, cynicism, because he thinks he can take advantage of the situation for an easy payday.

Joe moves into Norma's mansion to rewrite the script, and he becomes lovers with the significantly older woman. He quickly becomes accustomed to her extravagant lifestyle and all the luxuries it affords him. Meanwhile he begins a working relationship with Betty, a young script reader at Paramount. She likes one of his script ideas and thinks that together they can rewrite it and finish a screenplay with real depth. At night, Joe sneaks out

[114]

of Norma's mansion and meets with Betty as they feverishly work on their script.

Joe's TRIUMPH is at 1:29:44–1:29:55 (75% into the running time): <u>he's writing a meaningful script with Betty, and they're in love</u>. It meets both requirements for the TRIUMPH. It is (1) the ultimate manifestation of his SET-UP WANT of <u>a writing job</u>. And it's (2) his highest pinnacle of personal success. He's in love, and he's rediscovered fulfillment in his chosen profession, for the moment. He goes home to Norma's mansion, and in voice-over, Joe debates what to do about his love triangle.

Unlike the CRISIS in an Aristotelian comedy, where the protagonist is in between two bad options, in a tragedy at the TRIUMPH, the protagonist has two relatively good options. Joe's two good options are: to come clean to Betty about his relationship with Norma and hope that Betty forgives him, or to simply leave Norma now before Betty finds out about her. So which option does he choose? I'll reveal that in the next chapter, "Climactic Choice."

See the chart on the next page, where I show some tragic protagonists' SET-UP WANTs and how the WANTs ultimately manifest in the protagonists' TRIUMPHs.

Over Act 2, the tragic protagonist has seen their fortune rise. Their TRIUMPH at the 75% point is both their highest moment of success and the supreme iteration of their SET-UP WANT. They have everything they ever wanted and then some. But "be careful what you wish for"! Because after they reach their highest point, there's only one direction left to go . . .

Tragedies: Set-Up Wants and Their Corresponding Triumphs

FILM	SET-UP WANT	TRIUMPH
One Flew over the Cuckoo's Nest (not Nutshelled)	Escape incarceration	He's going to break out of the mental ward tonight
Chinatown	A classy case	Thinks he's solved the case
The Shining (not Nutshelled)	A quiet place to write	He's written pages and pages
Annie Hall	To prove to himself that he and Annie shouldn't have broken up	They got back together and she had them promise they'll never break up again
The Usual Suspects	To see Keaton go down	Proves to Verbal that Keaton is Keyser Soze
Being John Malkovich	Money	As John Malkovich, he has everything: fame, riches, and Maxine
Memento	To find his wife's killer	Teddy gives him the name and location of the killer
The Social Network	To get into a final club	He's the CEO of his own "final club" with a million members

Chapter

12

CLIMACTIC CHOICE

The **CLIMACTIC CHOICE***:*

- is at the center of the Climax
- in a comedy is a move away from the protagonist's FLAW and toward the STRENGTH
- in a tragedy is a move furthering the FLAW and failing to move toward the STRENGTH

Also:

- it is a decision made directly from having been between a rock and a hard place at the CRISIS (comedy) or from having experienced the ultimate manifestation of the SET-UP WANT in the TRIUMPH (tragedy)
- if a great Climax is inevitable yet unexpected, the screenwriter should try to find a "banana" (an unexpected third choice)
- it is sometimes repeated in a few iterations in Act 3

Film Nutshells Discussed in This Chapter

Collateral

Casablanca

Tootsie

Argo

Silver Linings Playbook

Little Miss Sunshine

Sunset Blvd.

Up in the Air

Chinatown

Annie Hall

The Usual Suspects

Being John Malkovich

Memento

The Social Network

AT THE END OF ACT 2, around the 75% point in a film or script, the protagonist will have been either at their CRISIS (comedy) or at their TRI-UMPH (tragedy). In either case, the protagonist now begins Act 3, when they will immediately face a big decision. And this decision is central to your story's Climax. At the heart of a true Climax, the protagonist is making a CLIMACTIC CHOICE.

The CLIMACTIC CHOICE is also the beginning of a reversal of fortune. In an Aristotelian comedy, the protagonist was just at their all-time low at the CRISIS, and the CLIMACTIC CHOICE is a first step toward positive change that will culminate in their usually happy ending at the very end. In a tragedy, the protagonist was just at their all-time high at the TRI-UMPH, and the CLIMACTIC CHOICE is a step in the wrong direction—the beginning of the downfall that will culminate in their usually sad ending.

Let's look at how the CLIMACTIC CHOICE works in Aristotelian come-dies first. In Act 2, various obstacles and the protagonist's own FLAW have driven the protagonist lower and lower, until at the CRISIS they should be forced into a corner, with no good options in sight.

In *Collateral*, protagonist Max has been essentially held hostage by hired killer Vincent, who forces Max to drive him around Los Angeles while

Vincent carries out five hits. Max's FLAW is his <u>inability to act</u>. This same FLAW is why he has been in what he calls his "temporary job" as a cab driver for 12 years, dreaming of someday starting a limousine company and never having made a single move toward it. And this FLAW has made the situation with Vincent worse and worse. Max's FLAW, his <u>inability to act</u>, means that Vincent has carried out his hits unimpeded. Toward the end of Act 2, the FBI and the LAPD think Max is behind the hits (since his cab is seen leaving the crime scenes), and the one cop who believes Max is innocent is killed by Vincent. Vincent has one last hit to carry out, but Max has reached his lowest point, his CRISIS. He has no good options in sight. If he refuses to drive Vincent, Vincent will kill him. If he continues, he still is likely to be killed by Vincent or by the police (who think Max is the killer). So what does he choose to do? He makes the CLIMACTIC CHOICE <u>to fight back</u> by speeding up and aiming the cab straight for an embankment, which sends it careening in the air and flips it several times. Vincent crawls from the overturned, totaled vehicle and has to flee on foot to get to his next hit. The CLIMACTIC CHOICE is a step the protagonist takes away from their FLAW, Max's <u>inability to act</u>, and toward their STRENGTH in the end, which in Max's case is to be <u>proactive</u>.

It is said that a great Climax is both inevitable and unexpected.[1] That's quite a tall order, but it's what we aspire to as screenwriters. *Collateral* achieves this. It is unexpected: you never see the CLIMACTIC CHOICE of Max flipping his cab coming. And it's inevitable: having seen it, you can't imagine the movie any other way. (*Collateral* also has a wonderfully ironic CRISIS. Max's SET-UP WANT is <u>for the passenger to not want to leave his car</u>. His CRISIS? <u>He wants him *out* of the car</u>.)

The best way that I can explain how to find an inevitable yet unexpected Climax for your story is as follows. At the CRISIS you've put your protagonist in a corner, between two bad options, a rock and a hard place. So now they have to make a CLIMACTIC CHOICE. What do they choose—rock? Or hard place? The answer is neither. Instead they choose—banana! Banana: it's a third choice no one saw coming. It's not a rock or mineral; it's not even in the same category. So when trying to find your inevitable but unexpected Climax for your story, see if your protagonist can find a banana to choose from in their CLIMACTIC CHOICE.

The CLIMACTIC CHOICE is sometimes repeated a few times in succes-

Max makes the CLIMACTIC CHOICE to fight back by intentionally crashing his cab in the film's "unexpected, yet inevitable" Climax. Still from *Collateral*. Copyright 2004, Dreamworks LLC and Paramount Pictures Corporation.

sion in the beginning of Act 3. In *Collateral*, Max's CLIMACTIC CHOICE is to fight back, and he does this four times, one after another by (1) flipping the cab over, (2) warning Annie, (3) saving Annie, and (4) killing Vincent. Likewise in *Casablanca*, Rick's CLIMACTIC CHOICE is to stick his neck out and go against his own self-interest to ensure that Laszlo and Ilsa get away, and he does this four times by (1) pulling a gun on Renault, (2) pushing Ilsa away and insisting that she get on the plane with Laszlo, (3) telling Laszlo that Ilsa never loved him (Rick), and (4) shooting Major Strasser.

Let's look at the CLIMACTIC CHOICE in *Tootsie*. Michael Dorsey's FLAW that he doesn't respect women has made his experience playing the female character on the soap opera more and more unpleasant until it's unbearable to him. He has a crush on co-star Julie, and at one point makes a pass at her while in disguise as Dorothy. Julie decides that if she were to continue their friendship, she would be leading Dorothy on. At the CRISIS at the end of Act 2, Julie says she can't be friends anymore, and he wants *out of the job* (86–87%: 1:40:08–1:41:17). But the soap opera producers have him in an ironclad contract to be on the soap for another year. Michael appears to be forced into a corner with no good options. He's between a rock and a hard place. His agent says there's no way they can get him out of his contract. But if he has to stay on the soap opera he'll be working with Julie every day, and that seems unbearable.

It was established earlier in the film that sometimes things are so last minute at the soap opera that occasionally they have to broadcast the soap live, because there is no time to pre-tape it. This happens at the beginning of Act 3, and Michael takes advantage of it to make his CLIMACTIC CHOICE: <u>live on the air, he reveals he's a man</u>. In character as the soap opera is broadcast live, he pulls off his wig and ad-libs, saying his female character is actually a male character in disguise. Everyone working on the soap opera and everyone watching on TV all discover in this moment that Michael is actually a man.

While you probably never saw this "banana" of his on-air revelation coming, it didn't come out of nowhere. Often there are banana tree seeds thrown out, usually at the beginning of Act 2 (such as when Michael was told that sometimes they have to broadcast the soap opera live). In trying to find a banana for your Act 3 CLIMACTIC CHOICE, look back in your script and see if inadvertently you've already sown some banana tree seeds you can use.

Another interesting thing about the CLIMACTIC CHOICE in *Tootsie* is that it uses a device known as Tell The Universe. Tell The Universe is not always the CLIMACTIC CHOICE, but it is a popular device to use for it. If at around 1:30:00 in a film the protagonist has a captive audience and is willing to go for broke, you may be about to see the protagonist Tell The Universe. Maybe the protagonist is live on the air (*Tootsie*). Or has the attention of Congress (*Mr. Smith Goes to Washington* [not Nutshelled]). Or both (*Dave* [not Nutshelled]). Or has the attention of the entire student body (*Crazy Stupid Love* [not Nutshelled], *Mean Girls* [not Nutshelled], *In and Out* [not Nutshelled], *Napoleon Dynamite* [not Nutshelled]). Or the dance contest is about to begin (also *Napoleon Dynamite*, *Silver Linings Playbook*, *Little Miss Sunshine*). All of these are variations of Tell The Universe. It can make for a great banana of a CLIMACTIC CHOICE.

The CLIMACTIC CHOICE is not typically a saintly change of behavior. The protagonist's flawed approach to life hasn't been working for them in Act 2 to the point where they have finally been driven into a corner, and now the screenwriter is going to force them to make a tough CLIMACTIC CHOICE in a different direction. But that CLIMACTIC CHOICE is not likely to represent a complete about-face of their flawed ways. The CLIMACTIC CHOICE is only a first step away from the FLAW and toward the STRENGTH. The full lesson has not been learned yet. It's only halfway toward change.

[121]

In *Tootsie*, when Michael makes his CLIMACTIC CHOICE (<u>reveals he's a man</u>), does his love interest, Julie, run up and embrace him and go off with him? No, quite the contrary. What she does instead is punch him in the stomach. He doesn't deserve to get the girl, not yet. His CLIMACTIC CHOICE is a move in the right direction; it's the beginning of change (telling the truth is better than lying). But it's only a first step toward change. Julie deserves more. He's going to have to make another move in the FINAL STEP to demonstrate that he has truly changed from the FLAW to the STRENGTH in order to get his happy ending.

The CLIMACTIC CHOICE comes directly out of being trapped between a rock and a hard place in the CRISIS. It's typically in the next scene after the CRISIS, or even in the same scene. Occasionally I see a film in which there are a few scenes after the CRISIS and before the CLIMACTIC CHOICE is made, but even in these instances the CLIMACTIC CHOICE is still a direct response to the CRISIS. In *Argo*, for example, the CRISIS is at 1:16:44–1:17:43 (64–65%), when <u>his boss tells him the mission is off</u>. Tony is in between a rock and hard place. He feels responsible for the six Americans and is convinced that they will be taken by the Iranians if he abandons the mission. But he has orders that the mission is off, and even if he were to defy orders, he would need CIA support to get through the airport. There appear to be no good options.

Before he makes his CLIMACTIC CHOICE, he confers with the Canadian ambassador, who suggests that the six Americans might panic if they are told the mission is off and that it would be best if Tony just not show up in the morning. We see the six drink in celebration as they burn the last of any documentation they would have left behind. We see Tony drinking and smoking alone in his hotel room. In the morning, the six gather with their luggage in the embassy foyer, nervously waiting. Tony looks through the fake passports that he is supposed to burn. And then at 1:22:23 he makes his CLIMACTIC CHOICE. He picks up the phone and <u>he tells his boss he's responsible for them and he's defying orders</u>, and he hangs up.

Although there are almost five on-screen minutes between the CRISIS and the CLIMACTIC CHOICE, Tony's CLIMACTIC CHOICE in the morning is a direct response to his CRISIS the night before. Essentially the CLIMACTIC CHOICE is a continuation of the phone conversation between Tony and his boss that began at the CRISIS. Tony needed the night to come to the decision to defy orders and to take the chance that CIA support would still get him through the airport. It's preferable for the CLIMACTIC CHOICE to immediately follow the CRISIS, but if absolutely necessary you can have a few additional scenes in between them. Any more than that and you risk losing the connection that the protagonist is making a CLIMACTIC CHOICE specifically because of the rock and the hard place that they are stuck between in the CRISIS.

The SET-UP WANT is always the opposite of the CRISIS in a comedy. The CLIMACTIC CHOICE in a comedy is also often opposed to the SET-UP WANT, but this is not always the case. *Collateral's* Max and *Tootsie's* Michael both make a CLIMACTIC CHOICE in order to get out of their SET-UP WANTs (for the passenger to not want to leave his car and a job, respectively). But I see many exceptions to this, and so I do not consider opposition to the SET-UP WANT a requirement for the CLIMACTIC CHOICE. In *Argo*, for example, Tony Mendez's SET-UP WANT is a plan to get the six Americans out of Iran. In his CLIMACTIC CHOICE he doesn't oppose his SET-UP WANT of a plan to get the six Americans out of Iran. Instead he furthers his SET-UP WANT in his CLIMACTIC CHOICE: he tells his boss he's responsible for them and he's defying orders. What is essential for the CLIMACTIC CHOICE in a comedy is that it is a step away from the FLAW and toward the STRENGTH.

Make sure that in determining your protagonist's CLIMACTIC CHOICE you don't put them between a rock and a soft place. If their CLIMACTIC CHOICE is between Cake or Death, your reader will know they're going to choose Cake, or find it highly unrealistic if they choose Death. Also problematic would be if your protagonist's CLIMACTIC CHOICE is between Death or Maybe Not Death. Which do you think they're going to choose? Obviously they'll try Maybe Not Death.

In a comedy at the CRISIS, the protagonist is between two bad options, a rock and a hard place. In the CLIMACTIC CHOICE, the protagonist is going to choose banana; that is, find an unexpected third choice. And this CLIMACTIC CHOICE will be a step in the right direction: away from their FLAW and toward the STRENGTH.

In a tragedy at the TRIUMPH, however, the protagonist is usually between two good options. In the CLIMACTIC CHOICE, the tragic protagonist won't choose one of their good options. Nor will they choose to move away from their FLAW and toward the STRENGTH. Instead, they will make a CLIMACTIC CHOICE that furthers their flawed ways and that fails to move toward the STRENGTH.

For example, in *Sunset Blvd.*, Joe's TRIUMPH is <u>he's writing a meaningful script with Betty and they're in love</u> (75%: 1:29:44–1:29:55). It's the ultimate manifestation of his SET-UP WANT, <u>a writing job</u>. And it's his highest moment of personal success. He's rediscovered fulfillment in his work as a writer, and he's in love. In his bliss he seems to have temporarily forgotten his FLAW, <u>cynicism</u>. But soon enough, it will rear its ugly head.

He goes home to Norma's mansion, and in voiceover, Joe debates what to do about his love triangle. He thinks up two good options: to come clean to Betty about his relationship with Norma and hope that Betty forgives him, or to simply leave Norma now before Betty ever finds out about her. Either one of these options could have worked. Each required just one thing: <u>faith</u>. It's the STRENGTH that's the opposite of his FLAW, <u>cynicism</u>. If he just had a little <u>faith</u> that Betty would forgive him or that things would work themselves out, either one of these options probably would have worked and given him a way out of his dilemma.

Joe's inner debate is interrupted when he discovers Norma on the phone. She has called Betty and is taunting her about not knowing with whom Joe lives. Joe's FLAW of <u>cynicism</u> completely overtakes him. Even though his two good options are still viable, he makes the self-sabotaging CLIMACTIC CHOICE <u>to rub his cynicism in Betty's face</u>. He grabs the phone, gives Betty the address, and tells her to come see for herself where he lives. When she arrives, he shows her the mansion's extravagances and explains the arrangement as "an older women who's well-to-do. A younger man who's not doing too well. Can you figure it out?" "No!" Betty says, trying to give him an out and denying everything she's just seen and heard. "I haven't heard any of this. I never got those telephone calls, and I've never been in this house. Now get your things together and let's get out of here," she says. He could still potentially have a positive outcome if only he would listen to her. But he doesn't listen; he keeps cruelly forcing Betty to see just how sordid his living situation is, and finally he shows her to the door, never to see her again.

A great example of a contemporary tragedy is *Up in the Air.* It's considered to be in the genre of romantic comedy, and watching it the first time,

[124]

I assumed it would be an Aristotelian comedy, too. Then midway through Act 2, I realized something: things were going too well. If this were actually an Aristotelian comedy, things would be going badly for the protagonist in Act 2. But for protagonist Ryan Bingham (George Clooney), things are going great in Act 2. And it dawned on me: this is no comedy; it's a tragedy! Things are going to go up and up, and the protagonist is going to hit his highest point, his TRIUMPH, and in Act 3 everything is going to come crashing down. And that's exactly what happens.

At his TRIUMPH at 1:30:26–1:31:20 (83%), he is about to give his "life in a backpack" motivational speech, this time at a Tony Robbins–level conference. He's at his highest moment of success, and his personal life is great, too. He's in a "no strings attached" relationship with an amazing woman who totally "gets" him. He's got nothing but good options in front of him.

But instead of savoring his success, what CLIMACTIC CHOICE does he make? He walks out mid-speech and surprises Alex—the woman he's been seeing—and discovers she has kids and a husband. He's shocked to find she has a family. It's a CLIMACTIC CHOICE that reflects his FLAW of hubris. Why else would he think it was okay to show up unannounced on her doorstep? They had a "no strings attached" relationship. Only someone with great hubris would assume that she must necessarily desire more from him. She is so lucky, Ryan seems to think; she is going to be wowed by my sweeping her off her feet.

Had *Up in the Air* been an Aristotelian comedy, we would have seen him in the CLIMACTIC CHOICE move away from his FLAW of hubris and toward the STRENGTH of humility. While the result of his CLIMACTIC CHOICE could certainly be described as humiliating, that is not at all the same thing as learning the STRENGTH of humility. On the contrary, this humiliating experience will ensure that he will likely never trust a woman again.

This lack of trust combined with his lack of the STRENGTH of humility means he will probably be incapable of ever making himself vulnerable, a requirement for forming a true connection with another. Having failed to overcome his FLAW of hubris, he seems doomed to a fate of living his whole life in his metaphoric backpack: that is, having no baggage but also never forming any ties.

In the chart on the next page, I look again at the tragedies from the pre-

[125]

Tragedies: How the Flaw Colors the Climactic Choice and Begins the Downfall

FILM	SET-UP WANT	TRIUMPH	FLAW	CLIMACTIC CHOICE
One Flew over the Cuckoo's Nest (not Nutshelled)	Escape incarceration	He's going to break out of the mental ward tonight	Hubris	Pays a hooker to sleep with Billy Bibbit before he goes
Chinatown	A classy case	Thinks he's solved the case	Doesn't know when to quit	Confronts everyone for the truth
The Shining (not Nutshelled)	A quiet place to write	He's written pages and pages	Thinks the isolation will be good for him	When his wife discovers the pages contain only one sentence repeated, he tries to bash her brains in
Annie Hall	To prove to himself that he and Annie shouldn't have broken up	They got back together and she had them promise that they'll never break up again	Self-absorbed	After her concert, a famous producer invites them to a party, but he says "we have that thing"
The Usual Suspects	To see Keaton go down	Proves to Verbal that Keaton is Keyser Soze	Arrogant	Lets Verbal leave
Being John Malkovich	Money	As John Malkovich, he has everything: fame, riches, and Maxine	Pride	He abandons Malkovich, hoping this will prove his love to Maxine
Memento	To find his wife's killer	Teddy gives him the name and location of the killer	Denial	Writes on Teddy's Polaroid "don't believe his lies"
The Social Network	To get into a final club	He's the CEO of his own "final club" with a million members	Hubris	He cheats his best friend in the new deal

Ryan's (George Clooney) ill-advised CLIMACTIC CHOICE to show up uninvited on his lover's doorstep. Still from *Up in the Air*. Copyright 2009, DW Studios LLC and Cold Springs Pictures.

vious chapter. This time I state the protagonists' respective FLAWs and the CLIMACTIC CHOICEs that further their FLAWs. Notice how in each instance the tragic protagonist had the ultimate manifestation of their SET-UP WANT in their TRIUMPH. See also how their FLAW colors their CLIMACTIC CHOICE, making it a step in the wrong direction and the beginning of their tragic downfall.

The CLIMACTIC CHOICE is what your whole story has been building toward. Human nature is such that it takes a CRISIS or a TRIUMPH to force someone to finally face their FLAW (or not). As Act 3 begins, it has all come to this moment. How will your protagonist's FLAW affect their CLIMACTIC CHOICE? What is your protagonist made of? They must confront their most important decision of the story. Now is the time to give your audience the big payoff.

Will your protagonist choose rock? Or will they choose hard place? Or are they fortunate enough to have two good options, both of which they'll throw away?

Find the unexpected but inevitable CLIMACTIC CHOICE. Find the banana for your protagonist!

Chapter

13

FINAL STEP

The **FINAL STEP***:*

- is the protagonist's last significant scene in the screenplay or film
- in a comedy is a second move away from the protagonist's FLAW and toward the STRENGTH in a new and different manner than in the CLIMACTIC CHOICE, completing the story's resolution and the protagonist's transformation
- in a tragedy is a second move furthering the protagonist's FLAW and failing to move toward the STRENGTH, completing the story's resolution and the protagonist's failure at self-transformation

Also:

- often significant time has passed between the CLIMACTIC CHOICE and the FINAL STEP

Film Nutshells Discussed in This Chapter

Casablanca

Argo

Being John Malkovich

ACT 3 IS KNOWN AS THE RESOLUTION. The beginning of Act 3, the Climax, is sometimes called the False Resolution. In it, in a comedy, the protagonist makes a CLIMACTIC CHOICE that represents a substantial move away from their FLAW and toward their STRENGTH (in a tragedy, the CLIMACTIC CHOICE is a move that furthers the FLAW and fails to move toward the STRENGTH). Sometimes the CLIMACTIC CHOICE is repeated a few times with similar actions until the full Climax plays out. But all these actions add up to only partial change on the part of the protagonist in a comedy (or failure to change in a tragedy); hence it's known as the False Resolution. The story is not yet resolved.

This is why the protagonist needs to make a second, separate move away from the FLAW and toward the STRENGTH before they'll achieve their usually happy ending in a comedy (in a tragedy, the protagonist makes a second move that fails to move away from the FLAW and toward the STRENGTH, which yields their usually sad ending). This second move I call the FINAL STEP. Let's look at how it works in Aristotelian comedies first.

The FINAL STEP is the protagonist's last significant scene(s) in the screenplay or film. It takes place after the dust has settled from the CLIMACTIC CHOICE and often after significant time has passed. In a comedy, the FINAL STEP also moves away from the FLAW and toward the STRENGTH, like the CLIMACTIC CHOICE did, but it does so in a new and different manner.

In *Casablanca*, Rick's CLIMACTIC CHOICE is <u>to stick his neck out</u> and go against his own self-interest to ensure that Laszlo and Ilsa get away, and he does this four times in succession by (1) pulling a gun on Renault, [130] (2) pushing Ilsa away and insisting that she get on the plane with Laszlo, (3) telling Laszlo that Ilsa never loved him (Rick), and (4) shooting Major Strasser. This CLIMACTIC CHOICE reflects a step away from Rick's FLAW that he's <u>lost faith in humanity</u> and toward the STRENGTH he ultimately gains, <u>faith in humanity</u>. He sticks his neck out four times to ensure one goal: that the Laszlos escape Casablanca safely. Once their plane is aloft, his goal is complete. At the same time, he is giving up the love of his life a second time, sacrificing his own interests for the good of humanity.

But where is he after this CLIMACTIC CHOICE? Having made this sacrifice and losing the love of his life for a second time, he could potentially revert back into his bitter, cynical ways. Also, he's given the letters of transit away and now he is trapped in Casablanca, increasingly an unsafe place to be.

This is why we need the FINAL STEP to complete the story's Resolution. In a comedy, it's a second move away from the FLAW and toward the STRENGTH. Rick's FINAL STEP is <u>to join the Resistance with Renault</u>. His transformation—from someone who has the FLAW of having <u>lost faith in humanity</u> to someone whose STRENGTH is <u>faith in humanity</u>—is now complete. The film closes with Rick's famous line: "Louie, I think this is the beginning of a beautiful friendship," making it a definite comedy. Even though he lost the love of his life a second time, he has regained his spirit, and he is better off than if she had never shown up in his bar. Had she never shown up, I think he would have gone to his grave a bitter, loveless man. But *because* he went through this journey and faced her and chose to give her up the second time, he is a changed man. Now he will love again someday. His FINAL STEP shows he's completed this transformation.

In *Casablanca*, Rick's FINAL STEP happens immediately after his CLIMACTIC CHOICE. But it is more typical for some time to have passed between the CLIMACTIC CHOICE and the FINAL STEP. This is because the CLIMACTIC CHOICE is at the heart of the story's Climax. Usually the Climax needs to fully play out and the dust from it needs to settle, and *then* we need the protagonist to make a FINAL STEP to complete their journey and fully resolve the story in their last scene(s) of the film or screenplay.

In *Argo*, Tony's CLIMACTIC CHOICE is <u>he tells his boss he's responsible for them and he's defying orders</u>, which happens at 1:22:23–1:22:33. This moment is the beginning of the film's Climax: Tony attempting to get the six Americans through the Tehran airport, past Iranian customs officials, and onto a plane before detection. Ultimately, he's successful, and the plane lifts off almost 20 minutes later at 1:41:46. Then the dust needs to settle. The Americans hug and laugh on the plane as Tony smiles to himself. There is

Only after all the dust settles from the big Climax does Tony Mendez (Ben Affleck) reunite with his wife and family in the FINAL STEP. Still from *Argo*. Copyright 2012, Warner Bros. Entertainment, Inc.

celebration at the CIA and the Hollywood office. The six Americans are honored by the State Department. Television footage shows American officials giving credit for their rescue to the Canadians. Tony boxes up the Argo materials for classified archives. His boss tells him he's receiving the Intelligence Star, but since it's a classified ceremony, no one will know. His boss adds that President Carter said Tony was a great American. Tony's FINAL STEP, the last two scenes of the film, then begins at 1:48:59: <u>he reunites with his family</u>. He arrives at his wife's door, hugs her, and watches his son fall asleep in a room filled with sci-fi action figures and one "Argo" storyboard.

Now let's look at how the FINAL STEP works in a tragedy. Act 3 begins with the protagonist's CLIMACTIC CHOICE, and the story's full Climax then plays out. In *Being John Malkovich*, protagonist Craig's CLIMACTIC CHOICE is when Maxine is kidnapped and Lester says they will kill her if he doesn't leave Malkovich, so <u>he abandons Malkovich, hoping this will prove his love to Maxine</u>. This reflects his failure to change from his FLAW of <u>pride</u> to the STRENGTH of <u>humility</u>, because it is quite evident to the movie viewer that Maxine has no interest in Craig outside of Malkovich. Only his self-delusional <u>pride</u> would lead him to think this could possibly work to his advantage. Once he leaves, Lester and his crew all pile inside the portal into Malkovich, victorious. When Craig finds himself once again unceremoniously dumped on the side of the New Jersey Turnpike, there also are Maxine and Lotte. The two have reconciled, and, unsurprisingly, Maxine couldn't care less about Craig's sacrifice. Craig screams after Maxine that he's going to go back into Malkovich and kick Lester out, so that she'll want to be with him again if he's Malkovich.

In the next moment, an on-screen legend informs us that it's seven years later. Now Lester is in John Malkovich, and he tells an older, balding Charlie Sheen (playing himself) he's found a way for them to live forever. He shows him pictures of a little girl. Next is the last scene of the film: Craig is inside the soul of the little girl, the seven-year-old daughter of Maxine and Malkovich, and he looks out of the little girl's eyes to the unbearable sight of Maxine being affectionate with Lotte. In his FINAL STEP he tells himself, "look away!" as he tries, unsuccessfully, to get the child's eyes to move away, but he can't avoid the sight of Maxine and Lotte embracing. Now we find out he missed the window of opportunity to re-enter Malkovich and instead wound up trapped inside Malkovich's off-spring and is forced to witness his love Maxine with someone else. Due to his FLAW of pride, he cannot comprehend the futility of trying to control the child and is doomed to an endless, fruitless struggle, instead of learning the STRENGTH of humility and accepting his fate.

A jump forward in time between the CLIMACTIC CHOICE and the FINAL STEP is not uncommon. You, the screenwriter, want the full impact of the Climax and its CLIMACTIC CHOICE to be experienced before approaching the FINAL STEP. Let the dust settle from the Climax and allow that whole chapter to come to a close. Then show us where the protagonist is six months or so later. In the last scene of the screenplay, have them take a FINAL STEP to demonstrate another move, different from their CLIMACTIC CHOICE but also away from their FLAW and toward the STRENGTH, if it is a comedy (in a tragedy the FINAL STEP fails to move away from the FLAW and toward the STRENGTH).

Chapter

14

STRENGTH

The **STRENGTH**:

- is the exact opposite of the FLAW

In a comedy:

- the STRENGTH is what the protagonist learns in the end
- in both the CLIMACTIC CHOICE and the FINAL STEP, the protagonist will move away from the FLAW and toward the STRENGTH

In a tragedy:

- the STRENGTH is what the protagonist *fails to* learn in the end
- in both the CLIMACTIC CHOICE and the FINAL STEP the protagonist will *fail to* move toward the STRENGTH and instead will further their FLAW

Film Nutshells Discussed in This Chapter

Argo

Sunset Blvd.

Chinatown

Annie Hall

The Usual Suspects

Being John Malkovich

Memento

The Social Network

Collateral

Casablanca

Braveheart

Titanic

Pulp Fiction

The Godfather

Witness

WHETHER A FILM OR SCREENPLAY is a comedy or a tragedy is revealed by whether or not the protagonist learns and changes from the FLAW to the STRENGTH over the course of the story.

Like the FLAW, the Nutshell Technique's STRENGTH doesn't exist in a fixed place in the story's timeline. In an Aristotelian comedy, the protagonist will learn the opposite of their FLAW over the course of Act 3. Both the CLIMACTIC CHOICE and the FINAL STEP are moves the comedic protagonist makes away from their FLAW and toward the STRENGTH. The STRENGTH on the Nutshell Technique form is a statement of what it is the protagonist learns in the end.

In a tragedy, the protagonist will fail to learn the opposite of their FLAW. Both the CLIMACTIC CHOICE and the FINAL STEP are opportunities for the protagonist to move away from their FLAW and toward the STRENGTH, but they will fail to do so both times. Instead, they will make moves that continue in the direction of their FLAW.

If you are having trouble narrowing your protagonist's FLAW down to one thing, see if you can identify one primary STRENGTH that in the end they learned (comedy) or failed to learn (tragedy). The opposite of the sole STRENGTH should be the right Nutshell FLAW.

When filling out the Nutshell Technique form, make sure that the FLAW and STRENGTH are direct opposites. If not, you'll need to tweak the wording of one or both so that they are. This is crucial. A mismatched FLAW-STRENGTH pair will yield a confusing or vague message.

That is the problem we saw in *Argo*. The film suggests a couple of FLAWs for protagonist Tony Mendez: <u>values job over family</u>, "loner," and "feels overly responsible." *Argo* is an Aristotelian comedy because the protagonist changes and is better off in the end. In a comedy, we should see the protagonist move away from their FLAW and toward the STRENGTH in both the CLIMACTIC CHOICE and the FINAL STEP. Tony's CLIMACTIC CHOICE is <u>he tells his boss he's responsible for them and he's defying orders</u>. But this isn't moving away from any of his three possible FLAWs; it's furthering them (he <u>values job over family</u>, he's making a "loner" decision, and he "feels overly responsible"). In the FINAL STEP, <u>he reunites with his family</u>. It is suggested that he learned the STRENGTH of <u>values family</u>, although I don't think anyone would go as far to say that he "values family over job," which is the actual opposite of the FLAW of <u>values job over family</u>. Also it is unclear how or why he learned the STRENGTH of <u>values family</u>. The CLIMACTIC CHOICE had nothing to do with <u>values family</u>, and so it feels like it comes out of nowhere in the FINAL STEP.

If a story is a tragedy, the protagonist doesn't gain the STRENGTH in the end, but you should still identify on the Nutshell Technique form what STRENGTH it is they failed to gain. Imagine what the happier outcome would have been had they not failed to learn the opposite of their FLAW. The tragic protagonist may have failed to learn this STRENGTH, but the screenplay reader or the movie audience will be the ones who learn it through seeing the protagonist's failure.

In *Sunset Blvd.*, for example, Joe Gillis seems to briefly put aside his FLAW of <u>cynicism</u> at his TRIUMPH: <u>he's writing a meaningful script with Betty and they're in love</u> (75%: 1:29:44–1:29:55). Somehow this hack screenwriter has found passion—for his chosen profession and for someone else. He has a dilemma, though. He can't keep hiding his living situation from Betty. At his CLIMACTIC CHOICE, he has two decent options. He could come clean to Betty about his relationship with Norma and hope that she forgives him.

Or he could simply leave Norma and hope Betty never finds out about her. Either option probably would have worked in his favor. Each just required one thing: the STRENGTH of <u>faith</u>. If only he could move away from his FLAW of <u>cynicism</u> and have a little <u>faith</u>. His happier outcome was right in front of him! But in both his CLIMACTIC CHOICE and his FINAL STEP, his <u>cynicism</u> completely overtakes him and leads him directly to his ultimate demise.

In the chart on the next page, I list the tragedies I've been comparing. This time, I've added the protagonists' final outcomes in the endings of the films and the STRENGTHs they failed to learn. In the last column, I've speculated on their probable happy endings had they instead learned the STRENGTHs.

If you are writing a tragedy, it is important to identify the STRENGTH that could have turned everything around for your protagonist. While they may have had some back luck along the way, the tragic protagonist is largely responsible for their own sad ending. Had they learned the STRENGTH, they would have been much better off. Your reader should be able to easily imagine the happier outcome they would have had—like the happier outcomes imagined in the chart—had your protagonist simply moved away from the FLAW and toward the STRENGTH.

The chart on page 140 shows some Aristotelian comedies and their potentially tragic outcomes had the protagonists failed to learn the STRENGTHs. Here you can see what was at stake and the often dire consequences had the protagonists failed to learn the STRENGTHs. The happy ending achieved in each actual film was the direct result of the protagonist's transformation from the FLAW to the STRENGTH.

Thank you, Aristotle. Our stories have evolved over the centuries, but still at the heart of them all is whether our protagonist will overcome their FLAW and learn the STRENGTH, or not. That, quite simply, is central to the great stories that make great films.

Tragedies and Their Potentially Comedic Outcomes

FILM	FLAW	FINAL OUTCOME	STRENGTH THEY FAILED TO LEARN	POTENTIAL OUTCOME HAD THEY LEARNED THE STRENGTH
One Flew over the Cuckoo's Nest (not Nutshelled)	Hubris	Lobotomized and permanently brain-dead	Humility	After serving his time, freed and returned to his normal life
Chinatown	Doesn't know when to quit	Evelyn is killed and Cross gets away with murder	Knows when to quit	A romantic future with Evelyn
The Shining (not Nutshelled)	Thinks the isolation will be good for him	Frozen to death in maze	Isolation is not good for him	Alive with his family in the suburbs
Annie Hall	Self-absorbed	He lost the love of his life	Appreciates her needs	They stayed together
The Usual Suspects	Arrogant	He let a criminal mastermind go free	Humility	He figured out Verbal was making the story up
Being John Malkovich	Pride	Trapped in their child's soul	Humility	Living his own life, as just Craig
Memento	Denial	Has set himself up to never figure out the truth	Honest with self	Moved on with his life instead of hunting the killer he can never find
The Social Network	Hubris	Alone hitting "Refresh" hoping in vain his ex will accept his Friend Request	Humility	A little less money but a lot more friends

Aristotelian Comedies and Their Potentially Tragic Outcomes

FILM	FLAW	STRENGTH	FINAL OUTCOME	POTENTIAL OUTCOME HAD THEY FAILED TO LEARN THE STRENGTH
Collateral	Inability to act	Proactive	Kills Vincent and saves Annie	Both he and Annie killed by Vincent
Casablanca	Lost faith in humanity	Faith in humanity	Gets Laszlos out of Casablanca and joins Resistance	Allies lose World War II because Laszlo captured
Braveheart	Rage	Supreme courage	Withstands torture and becomes a martyred hero	Caves under torture, so there is no hero to inspire Scots to eventually win their freedom
Titanic	Cowardice	Bravery	Leaves snooty fiancé and lives an exciting, independent, long life	Married to a man she hates
Pulp Fiction	Part of the "tyranny of evil men"	To shepherd the weak	Retires and spares lives	Stayed a hit man, probably killed when Vincent is
The Godfather	Naiveté	Realism	Defeats the four families	Defeated by the four families
Witness	Loner	Values community	Goes back to his community and makes room for her suitor	He wouldn't fit in in Amish country; she wouldn't fit in in the city

Three

ADVANCED APPLICATION *of*
the NUTSHELL TECHNIQUE

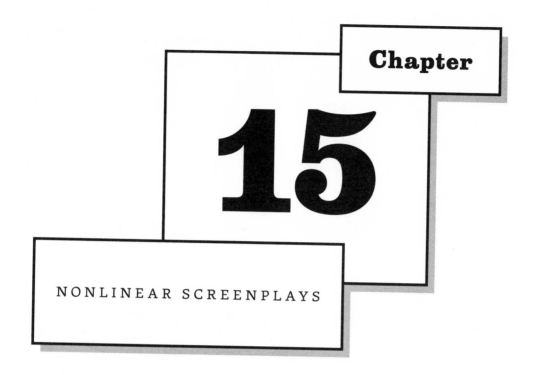

Chapter

15

NONLINEAR SCREENPLAYS

Film Nutshells Discussed in This Chapter

Pulp Fiction

THE NUTSHELL TECHNIQUE FORM and its elements correlate to specific points in the screenplay's page count and the film's running time, not to chronological time.

The protagonist's SET-UP WANT is evident in the protagonist's first dialogue scene in the screenplay or the film. It doesn't matter if this first scene is also the first chronological scene of the story or if it is actually a flashforward to the aftermath of the story we are about to see. The SET-UP WANT should be evident in this, the protagonist's first dialogue scene.

I included three true nonlinear films in this book: *Pulp Fiction*, *Memento*, and *Annie Hall*.[1] For all three films, if you were to re-edit them—cut them so that each told their respective tale in chronological order—the Nutshell would no longer work. The films are told out of chronological order for various reasons, but whatever those reasons are, the filmmakers still have the critical elements in the right places. Their story Nutshells work, whereas they would not if the stories were told in chronological order.

Let me walk through the Nutshell Technique applied to *Pulp Fiction* (see also my discussion of *Annie Hall* in "Film Nutshell Commentary" in Part 4).

I've heard a few screenwriting gurus claim that Butch (Bruce Willis) is the protagonist. He has a happy ending, so if he were the protagonist, the film would be an Aristotelian comedy. That would also mean he is the character who changes the most radically from their FLAW to their STRENGTH. I don't think he changes much. Yes, he rescues Marsellus. But this isn't the radical, 180-degree transformation from a FLAW to a STRENGTH that we should see in an Aristotelian comedy. It is circumstantial. He sees Marsellus suffering in such an extreme manner that it briefly awakes his empathy and stirs him to action. It isn't proof of true inner change. Also, Butch's story is completely self-contained in the middle section of the film. Of the five segments that make up *Pulp Fiction*, we could lop off three— "Prologue," "The Bonnie Situation," and "Epilogue"—plus the majority of a fourth ("Vincent Vega and Marsellus Wallace's Wife"), and Butch's story would be fully intact. If he's the protagonist, why even have the other four segments? They add nothing to Butch's story. It's my contention, therefore, that Butch is not the protagonist.

Jules (Samuel L. Jackson) is the protagonist. As you will see, he is the character who changes the most profoundly in this Aristotelian comedy.

Let's move past the SET-UP WANT and go straight to identifying the POINT OF NO RETURN, as we always do. The POINT OF NO RETURN is the scene where Jules confronts the young-looking "business associates" who have his boss Marsellus's briefcase. Jules terrorizes the main one, Brett, asking him what Marsellus looks like. "Is he a bitch?" he asks Brett. Brett answers, terrified, "No!" Jules retorts, "Then why you trying to fuck him like one?!" Then Jules recites the Bible verse he always says right before he kills someone, and he and Vincent shoot Brett dead.

The POINT OF NO RETURN is <u>Brett is trying to screw over Marsellus, so he kills him</u> (12–14%: 0:19:14–0:20:40).

So what's Jules's first-scene SET-UP WANT that he gets in this POINT OF NO RETURN? It's <u>to prevent Marsellus from being "fucked like a bitch."</u>

I'm inferring Jules's SET-UP WANT from what happens in the POINT OF NO RETURN. His job is to send a message by killing those who try to screw over his boss. In his first dialogue scene, Jules never says this SET-UP WANT out loud. In that scene, he and Vincent (John Travolta) are driving to Brett's, and Vincent is telling Jules about differences in Europe, such as a McDonald's quarter pounder being called a "royale with cheese." They are two co-workers having a watercooler moment, chatting about nothing important. While outwardly he's casually killing time on his commute, the fact is they are on their way to kill a man, something he cannot have forgotten. In this first scene, his SET-UP WANT <u>to prevent Marsellus from being "fucked like a bitch"</u> is certainly implied, if unspoken.

Jules's story is an Aristotelian comedy, which means he will reach his lowest point and the opposite sentiment or situation from his SET-UP WANT in the CRISIS. So what is his CRISIS? When is there the opposite sentiment or situation from his SET-UP WANT, <u>to prevent Marsellus from being "fucked like a bitch"</u>? That's right. At 1:41:50–1:44:57 (66–68%), <u>Marsellus is "fucked like a bitch," literally, when he is raped by Zed</u>.

Jules's whereabouts when this is happening aren't known to film viewers, and, presumably, he doesn't know it is happening. But this doesn't negate the fact that the opposite of Jules's SET-UP WANT <u>to prevent Marsellus from being "fucked like a bitch"</u> is being manifested in the CRISIS when <u>Marsellus is "fucked like a bitch," literally, when he is raped by Zed</u>. At the end of the film, when we realize that the rape scene was a jump forward in time and we put together the actual chronological order of events, we will realize that Jules probably retired as he said he would and was no longer in Marsellus's employment at the time of the rape. But this is information we do not know when the rape scene plays out on screen. And the fact of the matter, nonetheless, is that the opposite of Jules's SET-UP WANT manifests in the CRISIS whether he knows it or not.

After Marsellus's rape and the conclusion of Butch's story, the film jumps back in time and picks up back in Brett's apartment, right before Jules and Vincent kill him. Now we see that same sequence again but from a different point of view: another young "business associate" is holed up in a bathroom, listening, wild-eyed, with a huge gun drawn. Jules repeats his Bible verse "death sentence," and he and Vincent shoot and kill Brett, like we saw before. But this time the scene continues, and the armed business associate bursts out, gun blazing until he's used up all his bullets. Vincent and Jules look down in disbelief—not one of his many bullets hit

[145]

them—and they waste the business associate in three precise shots taken between them.

There is one irregularity with the *Pulp Fiction* Nutshell. The CATCH is supposed to happen immediately and directly with the POINT OF NO RETURN and therefore before Act 2. In *Pulp Fiction*, we actually see the POINT OF NO RETURN—<u>Brett is trying to screw over Marsellus, so he kills him</u>—two times. The first time is at 12–14% of the running time, at 0:19:14–0:20:40. The second time, at 1:31:04–1:54:36, plays out a bit longer to show us the business associate who bursts out shooting and Jules and Vincent reacting in disbelief that he missed every shot. Only this extended second version contains the CATCH: Jules <u>questions his line of work</u>. Normally Act 2 is largely about the CATCH testing the protagonist's FLAW, but, in the case of *Pulp Fiction*, the CATCH doesn't reveal itself until after Act 2 (Marsellus's rape is the CRISIS, which marks the end of Act 2).

Instead of the CATCH testing the FLAW in Act 2, the story digresses to two segments that have little to do with Jules. In the first, entitled "Vincent Vega and Marsellus Wallace's Wife," Jules makes one brief appearance when he and Vincent deliver Marsellus's briefcase to the bar (chronologically it's Jules's last scene). This segment culminates in Marsellus's wife overdosing on Vincent's heroin and Vincent saving her life by giving her a shot of adrenaline directly into her heart. The second segment is "The Gold Watch," Butch's story. This takes place presumably after Jules has retired, although we don't know this at the time; we only know that Jules is absent during most of Act 2. Normally in Act 2 we need the protagonist's FLAW to be tested by the CATCH in order to maintain conflict. Between the overdose, the shot to the heart, and Butch's story culminating in Marsellus's rape and rescue, screenwriter Quentin Tarantino certainly had no problem maintaining conflict without the CATCH testing the protagonist's FLAW as we normally need it to in Act 2.

So the CATCH and its test of the FLAW does not play out in Act 2 as it normally does, but instead in Act 3. The CATCH, that he <u>questions his line of work</u>, comes from the miracle Jules believes he witnessed. He thinks divine intervention saved his life and that God is telling him to consider his own moral worthiness as a hitman. The CATCH is the perfect test of his FLAW: he is <u>part of the "tyranny of evil men."</u> This is a phrase in his Bible verse death sentence that previously was meaningless to him. Before he

[146]

only said it because it sounded scary. But now that he believes God stopped the bullets from killing him, it has new meaning for him.

His CLIMACTIC CHOICE, to retire, comes quickly, before they have even left Brett's apartment. "From here on in, you can consider my ass retired," he declares to Vincent.

In the last scene of the film, Honey Bunny and Pumpkin have held up everyone in a diner. Pumpkin demands that Jules open Marsellus's briefcase. Jules does, and Pumpkin is mesmerized by the golden light emanating from it. Jules takes advantage of this moment and grabs Pumpkin's gun. He has completely taken control of the situation. But instead of killing them, Jules gives Pumpkin $1,500 and tells him he's buying something for it: his and Honey Bunny's lives. Instead of being part of the "tyranny of evil men," he's trying, he says, to shepherd the weak, which is the STRENGTH he learns in the end. He does this with his FINAL STEP: he lets Pumpkin and Honey Bunny go, sparing their lives.

Not only can the Nutshell Technique be used with nonlinear stories, often it is the reason why a story is told out of chronological order. The underlying principles of the Nutshell Technique—all of which come from the work of Aristotle—are more essential to the story than linear structure. As the filmmaker Jean-Luc Godard famously pointed out, a story should have a beginning, a middle, and an end, but not necessarily in that order.

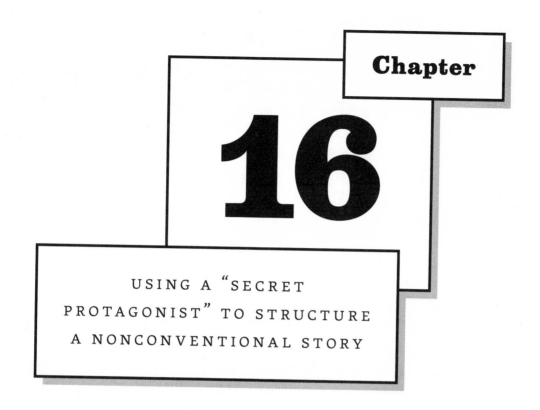

Chapter

16

USING A "SECRET PROTAGONIST" TO STRUCTURE A NONCONVENTIONAL STORY

Film Nutshells Discussed in This Chapter

Crimes and Misdemeanors

IF YOU ARE HAVING A HARD TIME getting the Nutshell Technique to work for your particular story, the problem (and solution) may lie in which character you designate as the protagonist.

If your protagonist doesn't learn the STRENGTH and move away from their FLAW, and yet your protagonist is *better off* in the end—rather than worse off, as they should be in a tragedy—you may have identified the wrong character as the protagonist.

Likewise, if your protagonist is worse off in the end but their own FLAW in no way contributed to their sad ending, this character may also have been misidentified as the protagonist.

Something to keep in mind, because it does happen on occasion, is that the "main character" may not be the protagonist. In other words, the protagonist isn't necessarily the character with the most lines of dialogue or on-screen time. In an Aristotelian comedy, the protagonist is the character who changes the most profoundly from their FLAW to learn its opposite, their STRENGTH, and they usually are better off; that is, they have a happy ending. In a tragedy, the protagonist is the character who *fails to* change from their FLAW and learn its opposite STRENGTH, and they usually are worse off; that is, they have a sad ending.

If the character you've identified as your protagonist doesn't follow one of these patterns, then look to see if perhaps another character does (or can be made to do so). This other character may be what I call a "secret protagonist." Designating a "secret protagonist" can be a useful technique for better structuring a story that doesn't appear to fit the Aristotelian models for comedy and tragedy.

Woody Allen's *Crimes and Misdemeanors* is a great example of using a "secret protagonist" to structure a story. It's a fantastic film (the best of Allen's dramas). It may be hard to find, but I recommend seeking it out if you want to see a great example of how to structure a story that doesn't seem to fit conventional models.

Most any synopsis of the film will describe Judah (Martin Landau) as the protagonist. He certainly has the most screen time; he pushes most of the action of the film forward; and we are on the edge of our seats at times following his plotline. He's a successful Manhattan ophthalmologist whose mistress Dolores (Anjelica Huston) wants to expose their affair to his wife, and he's desperate to find a way to stop her. He seeks the advice of a patient of his who is also a family friend, a rabbi named Ben (Sam Waterson). Ben is starting to lose his sight and is perhaps our second candidate for the film's protagonist. Ben counsels Judah to come clean to his wife. But Judah doesn't think his wife could possibly forgive him, and meanwhile his mistress escalates matters by threatening to also expose that Judah has embezzled from his business. So Judah pays a hit man, and Dolores is killed. Soon the police are questioning him, and we don't know if he will get caught in his lies or if the weight of his conscience will bring Judah to confess what he has done.

[150] If Judah is the protagonist and the story is a tragedy, he would have to be eventually brought down by his failure to learn that he's not above morality. If he's the protagonist and it's a comedy, we would see him learn and change and either turn himself in or find some other way to redeem

himself in our eyes. But neither happens. He isn't brought down, nor does he redeem himself. He gets away with murder. And we find out in the last scene that he has discovered that he doesn't even have any of the guilt or regret he thought he'd have. So despite the facts that Judah is the most prominent character, that he pushes most of the action forward, and that his plotline is the most important—and, in fact, is absolutely integral to the telling of *Crimes and Misdemeanors*—structurally speaking, he is not the protagonist.

As I mentioned, Ben the rabbi might be our second candidate for protagonist, although his plotline does move to the background after the first act. We see that he is a truly kind and moral man. While he counsels Judah that confessing to his wife would be the best course, he doesn't insist that Judah has to "do the right thing" or try to hold Judah up to Ben's or anyone else's moral code. When Judah lies and tells Ben that the mistress simply dropped the matter and the problem went away, Ben is genuinely happy for Judah. But while things only get better for Judah, they get worse for Ben. By the end of the film, Ben has gone completely blind, and we see him dancing with his daughter at her wedding, which has been paid for by someone else because Ben cannot afford it. Ben, however, has done nothing to contribute to his calamity.

For a story to be a tragedy, our hero *must* contribute to their tragic end. A tragedy is *not* bad things randomly happening to a character. A tragedy is by definition (Aristotle's) a protagonist failing to overcome their FLAW, failing to change, and therefore causing their own downfall and tragic end. Ben's storyline is a sad tale, indeed, but it is not a tragedy.

Our third candidate for protagonist would be Cliff (played by Woody Allen). He is only tangentially related to the main Judah and Ben plotlines, and he seems to be there mainly to provide (very welcome) comic relief to the film. He doesn't even cross paths with Judah until the very last scene of the film, when he meets him for the first time at Ben's daughter's wedding.

Cliff is a documentary filmmaker who falls for film producer Halley (Mia Farrow) while they work on a puff piece they're shooting about famous, pompous Hollywood director Lester (Alan Alda). Cliff's FLAW is that he's <u>idealistic</u>. He believes there should be Hollywood endings in life. This makes him blind (so to speak) to the fact that Halley isn't interested in him but instead, is interested in pompous Lester. At Cliff's TRIUMPH, <u>he</u>

Judah (Martin Landau) laughs at Cliff's (Woody Allen) insistence that you can't have a story where a guilty man gets away with murder. Still from *Crimes and Misdemeanors*. Copyright 1989, Orion Pictures Corporation.

kisses Halley. She tells him she's not ready, and he kisses her again (74–75%: 1:17:12–1:18:23). Cliff, in his idealization of the situation, isn't really hearing her. In his CLIMACTIC CHOICE, he proposes to Halley. She won't take him seriously and tells him she's going to Europe for a while.

Cliff doesn't see Halley again until the last scene, Ben's daughter's wedding, when she arrives, now married to his nemesis, Lester. Despondent, Cliff escapes outside the wedding for a moment, where he meets for the first time ophthalmologist Judah. Upon hearing Cliff is a filmmaker, Judah says he's got a great idea for film. Judah proceeds to tell Cliff his supposedly fictional tale about a successful man threatened with exposure by his mistress who then has her killed. And at the end of his fictional story, Judah says, instead of being wracked with guilt, instead of being brought to justice by the authorities, the man is guilt-free and has never been charged. The police pin the crime on a drifter who is in fact guilty of other murders anyway (so the man doesn't have to bear the guilt of knowing an innocent person is paying for the crime). Judah's "fictional" character finds himself completely safe from the fear of ever getting caught. The guilt he thought he was feeling lifts, and he feels even lighter than before, even better off than before it all happened. Cliff protests that you can't end a movie with a guilty man getting away with murder. He tells Judah that his "fictional" character should confess to his crimes. Judah laughs and says Cliff has seen too many movies, because in the real world, there are no Hollywood endings.

This is *exactly* what Cliff failed to learn and what makes him the story's tragic "secret protagonist": unlike in the movies, there aren't Hollywood endings in life. The sad truth is that in life there are bad people who get away with murder every day, and there are good people who have awful things happen to them for no justifiable reason. Life ain't fair. *That's* the tragedy. That Judah's plotline isn't a tragedy *is* part of the tragedy for Cliff.

So Cliff is the protagonist in *Crimes and Misdemeanors*, as far as Aristotle and I are concerned. No, he doesn't drive the action or make the hardest choices, which are what we typically expect of the protagonist. But Cliff is the character who provides the moral backbone, the Aristotelian trajectory as it were, and the other two candidates do not. Judah gets away with murder, unchanged and unscathed by the experience, so he can't be the protagonist. And unlike Ben, the rabbi who goes blind, Cliff contributes to his own tragic downfall. Cliff's metaphoric blindness to the fact that life doesn't have Hollywood endings causes him to miss the cues from Halley that she's not interested. Hearing Judah's "fictional" story about a man who gets away with murder just further cements his outrage. Instead of bucking up and facing reality and accepting life as it is, Cliff appears doomed to more misery and a life of self-pity.

Sometimes the only lens through which we can make sense of the fact that life isn't fair is through designating a "secret protagonist." We need it for a story to be palatable. Without it, it's too much of a downer. Life is just too cruel sometimes. Cliff's storyline may seem like a thin thread in the totality of *Crimes and Misdemeanors*, but it's the thread that holds the whole thing together and makes it work. It's the story's structural backbone and provides a relatable moral framework. Without Cliff, the story wouldn't work. Having a "secret protagonist" is a brilliant way to make work what appears to be story about a man who gets away with murder.

FILM NUTSHELLS

THIS SECTION CONTAINS NUTSHELL TECHNIQUE forms completed for 30 famous and otherwise noteworthy films, most of which have already been discussed in part.

Almost all the films included meet all the requirements of the Nutshell Technique Checklist. Exceptions are noted in the Film Nutshell Commentary that begins on page 190.

It pains me that only five of the films have a female protagonist, four if you don't count animated characters. Not only are there fewer films with female protagonists, there are even fewer *good* films with strong female characters.

Nutshell Technique Checklist: Comedy

Here is a checklist for the Nutshell Technique form for comedy. To properly set up a story, all of the following must be true:

☐ Does the protagonist get their SET-UP WANT immediately and directly in the POINT OF NO RETURN?

☐ Does the protagonist get something immediately in the POINT OF NO RETURN that they don't want, the CATCH?

☐ Is the CATCH the perfect test of their FLAW?

☐ Is the CRISIS the lowest the protagonist can go? (What if they were in jail? Or considering suicide?)

☐ In the CRISIS, is the protagonist in the exact opposite state of mind or situation of where they were in the SET-UP WANT?

☐ In both the CLIMACTIC CHOICE and the FINAL STEP, does the protagonist move away from the FLAW and toward the STRENGTH?

☐ Are the FLAW and the STRENGTH exact opposites?

Nutshell Technique Checklist: Tragedy

Here is a checklist for the Nutshell Technique form for tragedy. To properly set up a story, all of the following must be true:

☐ Does the protagonist get their SET-UP WANT immediately and directly in the POINT OF NO RETURN?

☐ Does the protagonist get something immediately in the POINT OF NO RETURN that they don't want, the CATCH?

☐ Is the CATCH the perfect test of their FLAW?

☐ Is the TRIUMPH the highest the protagonist can go?

☐ Does the protagonist get the ultimate manifestation of their SET-UP WANT in the TRIUMPH?

☐ In both the CLIMACTIC CHOICE and the FINAL STEP, does the protagonist fail to move toward the STRENGTH and instead further the FLAW?

☐ Are the FLAW and the STRENGTH exact opposites?

Annie Hall

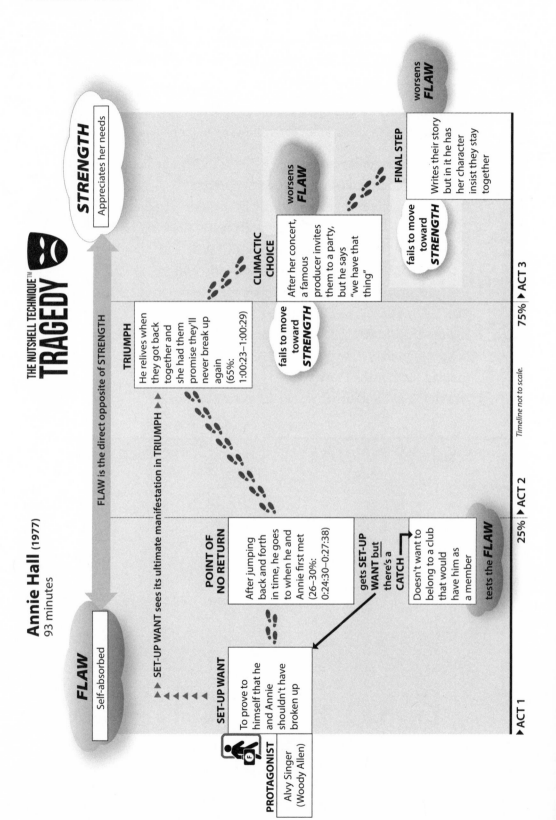

Annie Hall (1977)
93 minutes

THE NUTSHELL TECHNIQUE™
TRAGEDY

FLAW is the direct opposite of STRENGTH

▶▶ SET-UP WANT sees its ultimate manifestation in TRIUMPH ▶▶

FLAW
Self-absorbed

STRENGTH
Appreciates her needs

PROTAGONIST
Alvy Singer (Woody Allen)

SET-UP WANT
To prove to himself that he and Annie shouldn't have broken up

gets **SET-UP WANT** but there's a **CATCH**
Doesn't want to belong to a club that would have him as a member

tests the **FLAW**

POINT OF NO RETURN
After jumping back and forth in time, he goes to when he and Annie first met (26–30%: 0:24:30–0:27:38)

TRIUMPH
He relives when they got back together and she had them promise they'll never break up again (65%: 1:00:23–1:00:29)

fails to move toward **STRENGTH**

CLIMACTIC CHOICE
After her concert, a famous producer invites them to a party, but he says "we have that thing"

worsens **FLAW**

fails to move toward **STRENGTH**

FINAL STEP
Writes their story but in it he has her character insist they stay together

worsens **FLAW**

▶ ACT 1   25% ▶ ACT 2   75% ▶ ACT 3

Timeline not to scale.

Argo

THE NUTSHELL TECHNIQUE™ COMEDY

Argo (2012)
120 minutes

FLAW
Values job over family

STRENGTH
Values family

FLAW is the direct opposite of STRENGTH

PROTAGONIST
Tony Mendez (Ben Affleck)

SET-UP WANT
A plan to get the six Americans out of Iran

POINT OF NO RETURN
Planet of the Apes is on TV, and he gets an escape plan (19–20%: 0:22:44–0:24:15)

gets SET-UP WANT but there's a CATCH

It requires they look like a real film overnight

tests the FLAW

SET-UP WANT is the direct opposite of CRISIS

CRISIS

His boss tells him the mission is off (64–65%: 1:16:44–1:17:43)

away from FLAW

CLIMACTIC CHOICE

He tells his boss he's responsible for them and he's defying orders

toward STRENGTH

away from FLAW

FINAL STEP

He reunites with his family

toward STRENGTH

Timeline not to scale.

▶ ACT 1   25% ▶ ACT 2   75% ▶ ACT 3

August: Osage County

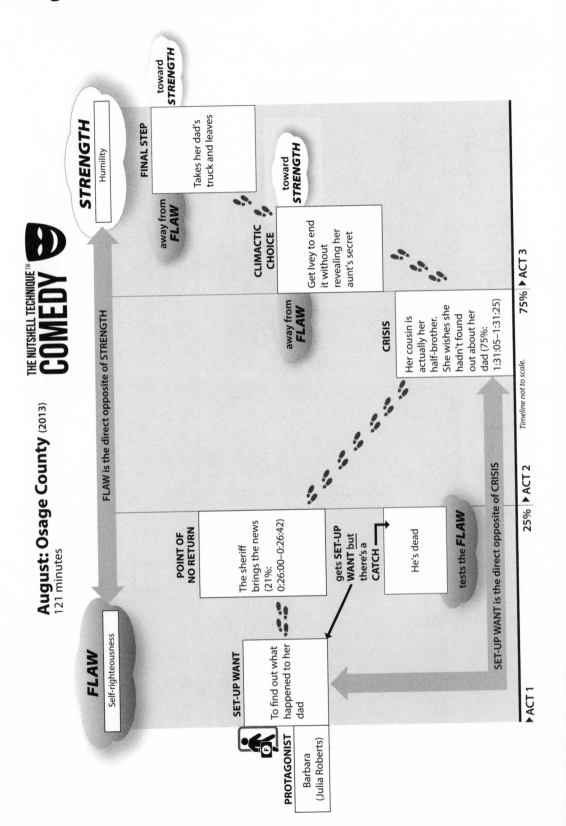

THE NUTSHELL TECHNIQUE™ COMEDY

August: Osage County (2013)
121 minutes

FLAW is the direct opposite of **STRENGTH**

STRENGTH

Humility

FLAW

Self-righteousness

FINAL STEP

Takes her dad's truck and leaves

toward **STRENGTH**

away from **FLAW**

CLIMACTIC CHOICE

Get Ivey to end it without revealing her aunt's secret

toward **STRENGTH**

away from **FLAW**

CRISIS

Her cousin is actually her half-brother. She wishes she hadn't found out about her dad (75%: 1:31:05–1:31:25)

POINT OF NO RETURN

The sheriff brings the news (21%: 0:26:00–0:26:42)

SET-UP WANT

To find out what happened to her dad

gets **SET-UP WANT** but there's a **CATCH**

He's dead

tests the **FLAW**

PROTAGONIST

Barbara (Julia Roberts)

SET-UP WANT is the direct opposite of **CRISIS**

▶ ACT 1   25% ▶ ACT 2   *Timeline not to scale.*   75% ▶ ACT 3

Being John Malkovich

Being John Malkovich (1999)
113 minutes

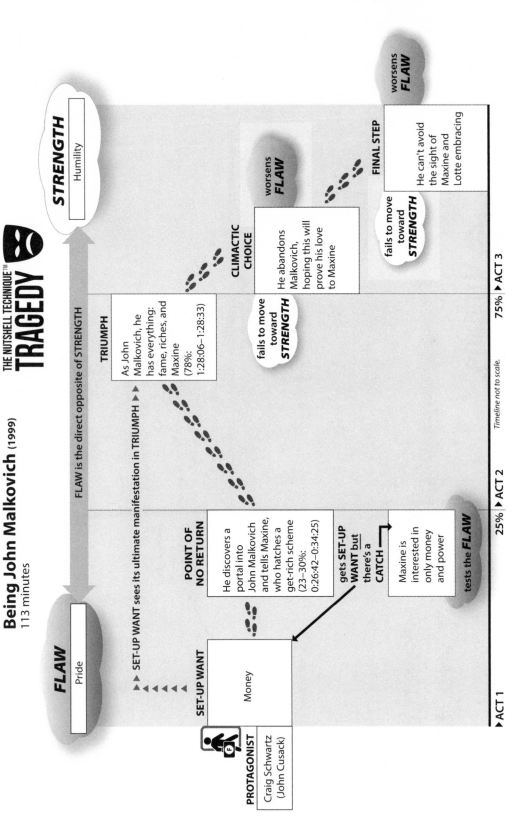

THE NUTSHELL TECHNIQUE™
TRAGEDY

FLAW
Pride

STRENGTH
Humility

FLAW is the direct opposite of STRENGTH

▶ SET-UP WANT sees its ultimate manifestation in TRIUMPH ▶

PROTAGONIST
Craig Schwartz (John Cusack)

SET-UP WANT
Money

POINT OF NO RETURN
He discovers a portal into John Malkovich and tells Maxine, who hatches a get-rich scheme (23–30%: 0:26:42–0:34:25)

gets SET-UP WANT but there's a CATCH

Maxine is interested in only money and power

tests the FLAW

TRIUMPH
As John Malkovich, he has everything: fame, riches, and Maxine (78%: 1:28:06–1:28:33)

fails to move toward STRENGTH

CLIMACTIC CHOICE
He abandons Malkovich, hoping this will prove his love to Maxine

worsens FLAW

fails to move toward STRENGTH

FINAL STEP
He can't avoid the sight of Maxine and Lotte embracing

worsens FLAW

▶ ACT 1   25% ▶ ACT 2   *Timeline not to scale.*   75% ▶ ACT 3

The Big Lebowski

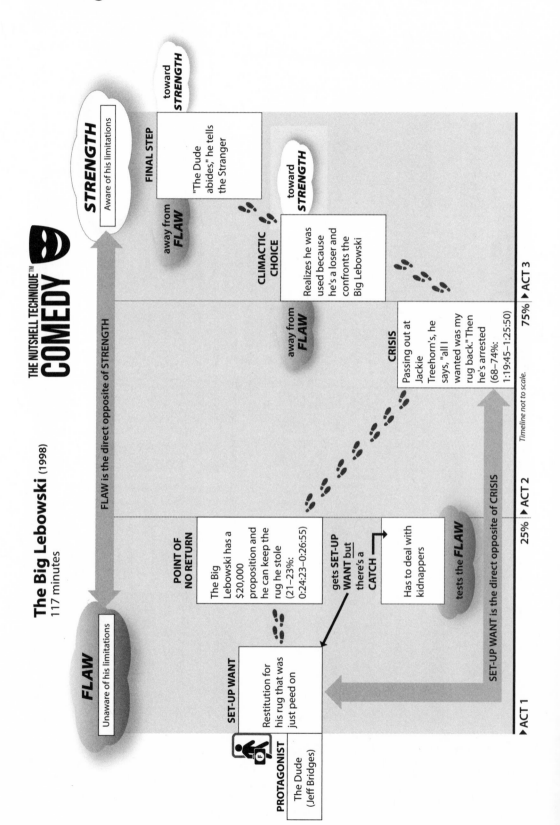

THE NUTSHELL TECHNIQUE™
COMEDY

The Big Lebowski (1998)
117 minutes

FLAW
Unaware of his limitations

FLAW is the direct opposite of STRENGTH

STRENGTH
Aware of his limitations

SET-UP WANT
Restitution for his rug that was just peed on

PROTAGONIST
The Dude (Jeff Bridges)

POINT OF NO RETURN
The Big Lebowski has a $20,000 proposition and he can keep the rug he stole (21–23%: 0:24:23–0:26:55)

gets SET-UP WANT but there's a CATCH
→ Has to deal with kidnappers

tests the **FLAW**

CRISIS
Passing out at Jackie Treehorn's, he says, "all I wanted was my rug back." Then he's arrested (68–74%: 1:19:45–1:25:50)

away from **FLAW**

CLIMACTIC CHOICE
Realizes he was used because he's a loser and confronts the Big Lebowski

toward **STRENGTH**

FINAL STEP
"The Dude abides," he tells the Stranger

away from **FLAW**

toward **STRENGTH**

SET-UP WANT is the direct opposite of CRISIS

▶ ACT 1   25% ▶ ACT 2   *Timeline not to scale.*   75% ▶ ACT 3

The Bourne Identity

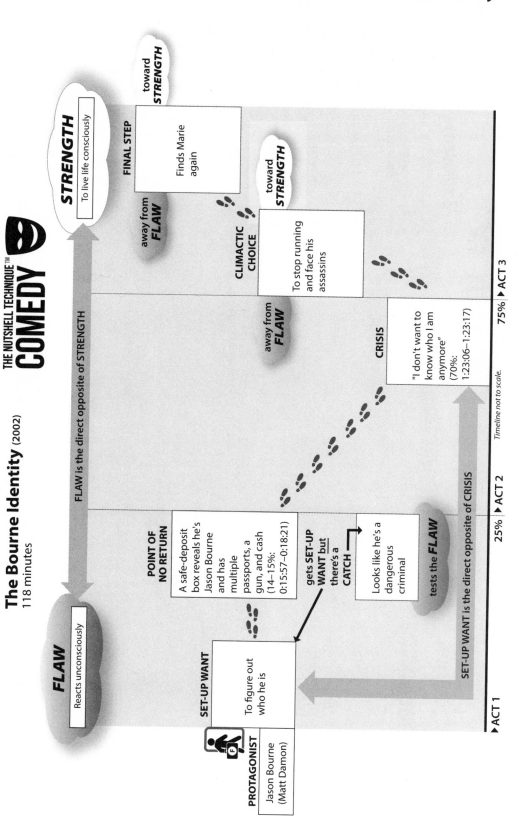

THE NUTSHELL TECHNIQUE™ COMEDY

The Bourne Identity (2002)
118 minutes

FLAW is the direct opposite of STRENGTH

FLAW
Reacts unconsciously

STRENGTH
To live life consciously

PROTAGONIST
Jason Bourne (Matt Damon)

SET-UP WANT
To figure out who he is

POINT OF NO RETURN
A safe-deposit box reveals he's Jason Bourne and has multiple passports, a gun, and cash (14–15%: 0:15:57–0:18:21)

gets SET-UP WANT but there's a CATCH
Looks like he's a dangerous criminal

tests the FLAW

SET-UP WANT is the direct opposite of CRISIS

CRISIS
"I don't want to know who I am anymore" (70%: 1:23:06–1:23:17)

away from FLAW

CLIMACTIC CHOICE
To stop running and face his assassins

toward STRENGTH

away from FLAW

FINAL STEP
Finds Marie again

toward STRENGTH

▶ ACT 1   25% ▶ ACT 2   75% ▶ ACT 3

Timeline not to scale.

Braveheart

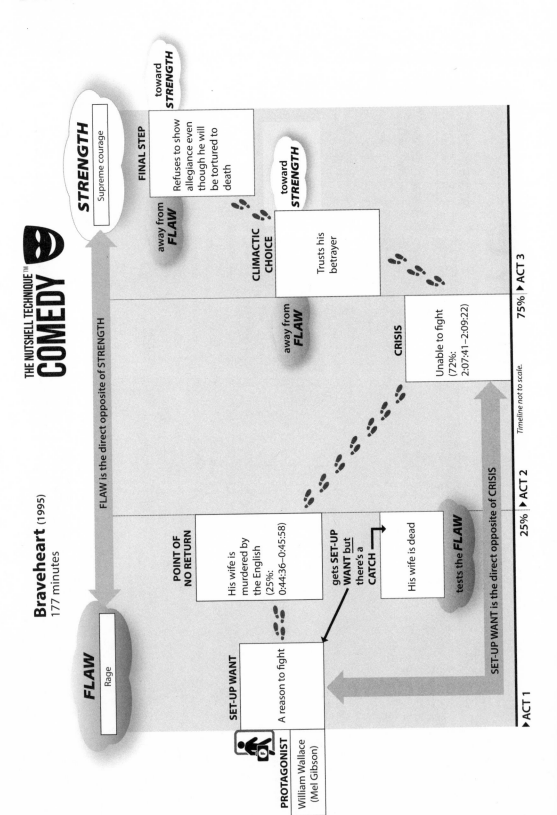

Braveheart (1995)
177 minutes

THE NUTSHELL TECHNIQUE™
COMEDY

FLAW is the direct opposite of STRENGTH

FLAW
Rage

STRENGTH
Supreme courage

PROTAGONIST
William Wallace (Mel Gibson)

SET-UP WANT
A reason to fight

gets **SET-UP WANT** but there's a **CATCH**
His wife is dead

tests the **FLAW**

POINT OF NO RETURN
His wife is murdered by the English (25%: 0:44:36–0:45:58)

FINAL STEP
Refuses to show allegiance even though he will be tortured to death

toward **STRENGTH**

away from **FLAW**

CLIMACTIC CHOICE
Trusts his betrayer

toward **STRENGTH**

away from **FLAW**

CRISIS
Unable to fight (72%: 2:07:41–2:09:22)

SET-UP WANT is the direct opposite of CRISIS

▶ ACT 1   25% ▶ ACT 2   75% ▶ ACT 3

Timeline not to scale.

Casablanca

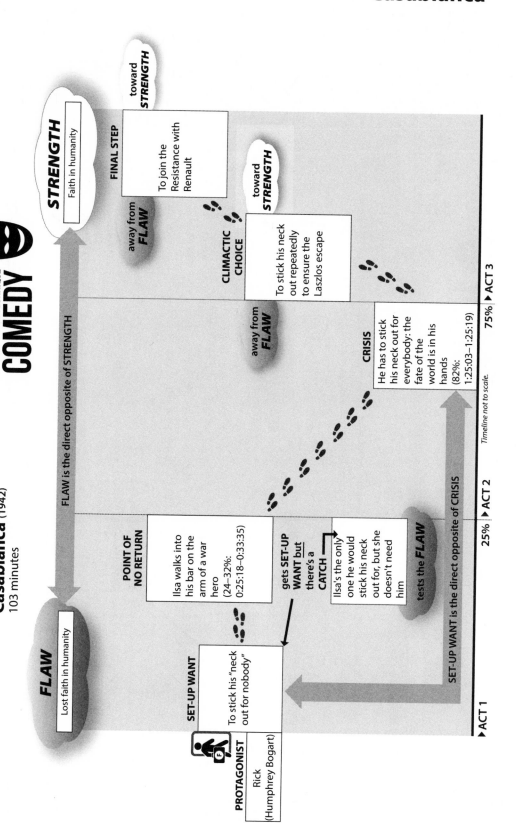

THE NUTSHELL TECHNIQUE™
COMEDY

Casablanca (1942)
103 minutes

FLAW
Lost faith in humanity

STRENGTH
Faith in humanity

FLAW is the direct opposite of STRENGTH

PROTAGONIST
Rick (Humphrey Bogart)

SET-UP WANT
To stick his "neck out for nobody"

gets SET-UP WANT but there's a CATCH

Ilsa's the only one he would stick his neck out for, but she doesn't need him

POINT OF NO RETURN
Ilsa walks into his bar on the arm of a war hero (24–32%: 0:25:18–0:33:35)

tests the *FLAW*

SET-UP WANT is the direct opposite of CRISIS

CRISIS
He has to stick his neck out for everybody: the fate of the world is in his hands (82%: 1:25:03–1:25:19)

away from *FLAW*

CLIMACTIC CHOICE
To stick his neck out repeatedly to ensure the Laszlos escape

toward *STRENGTH*

away from *FLAW*

FINAL STEP
To join the Resistance with Renault

toward *STRENGTH*

◀ ACT 1   25% ▶ ACT 2   75% ▶ ACT 3

Timeline not to scale.

Chinatown

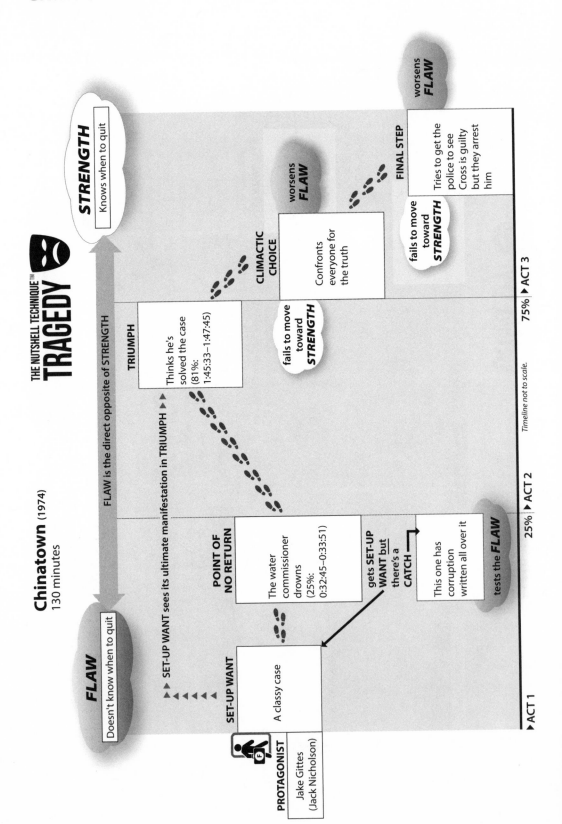

Chinatown (1974)
130 minutes

THE NUTSHELL TECHNIQUE™
TRAGEDY

FLAW
Doesn't know when to quit

FLAW is the direct opposite of STRENGTH

STRENGTH
Knows when to quit

▲ ▲ SET-UP WANT sees its ultimate manifestation in TRIUMPH ▲ ▲

PROTAGONIST
Jake Gittes
(Jack Nicholson)

SET-UP WANT
A classy case

gets SET-UP WANT but there's a CATCH
This one has corruption written all over it

tests the FLAW

POINT OF NO RETURN
The water commissioner drowns
(25%: 0:32:45–0:33:51)

TRIUMPH
Thinks he's solved the case
(81%: 1:45:33–1:47:45)

fails to move toward STRENGTH

CLIMACTIC CHOICE
Confronts everyone for the truth

worsens FLAW

fails to move toward STRENGTH

FINAL STEP
Tries to get the police to see Cross is guilty but they arrest him

worsens FLAW

▶ ACT 1   25% ▶ ACT 2   *Timeline not to scale.*   75% ▶ ACT 3

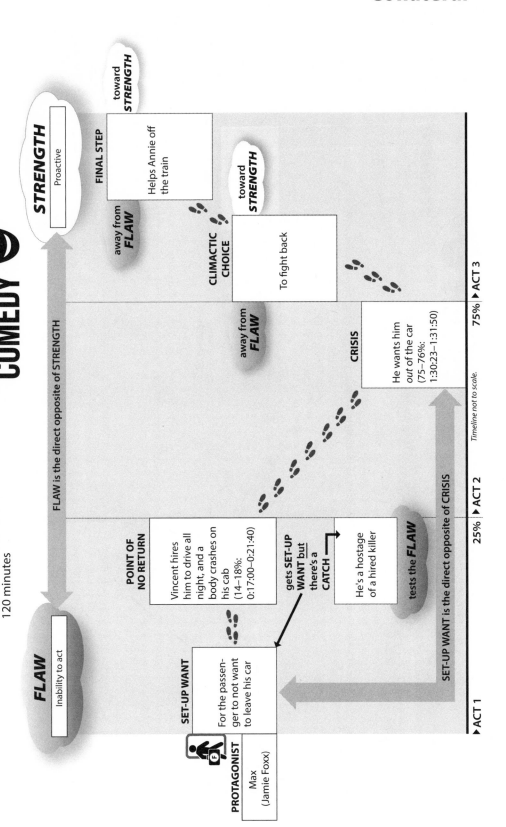

Collateral

THE NUTSHELL TECHNIQUE™ COMEDY

Collateral (2004)
120 minutes

FLAW
Inability to act

STRENGTH
Proactive

FLAW is the direct opposite of STRENGTH

PROTAGONIST
Max (Jamie Foxx)

SET-UP WANT
For the passenger to not want to leave his car

POINT OF NO RETURN
Vincent hires him to drive all night, and a body crashes on his cab
(14–18%: 0:17:00–0:21:40)

gets SET-UP WANT but there's a CATCH
He's a hostage of a hired killer

tests the FLAW

CRISIS
He wants him out of the car
(75–76%: 1:30:23–1:31:50)

away from FLAW

CLIMACTIC CHOICE
To fight back

away from FLAW

FINAL STEP
toward STRENGTH
Helps Annie off the train

toward STRENGTH

SET-UP WANT is the direct opposite of CRISIS

Timeline not to scale.

▶ ACT 1   25% ▶ ACT 2   75% ▶ ACT 3

Crimes and Misdemeanors

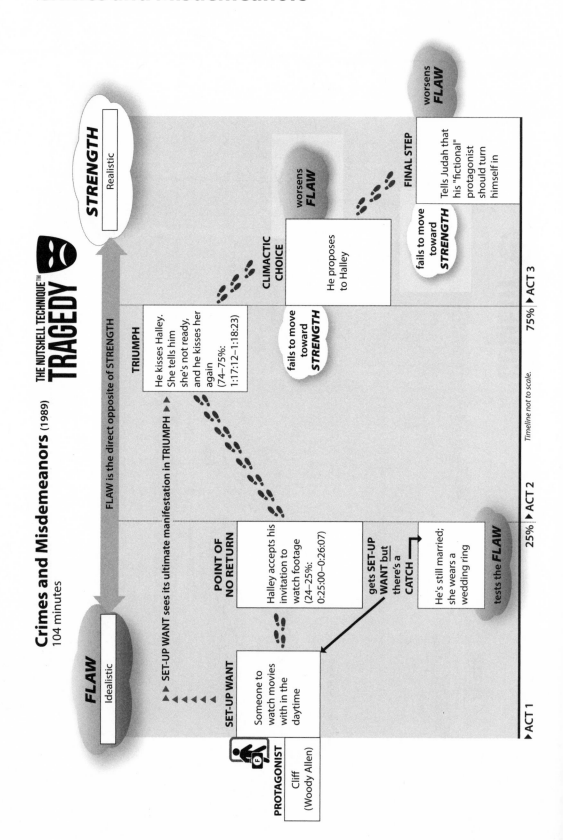

THE NUTSHELL TECHNIQUE™
TRAGEDY

Crimes and Misdemeanors (1989)
104 minutes

PROTAGONIST
Cliff (Woody Allen)

FLAW
Idealistic

STRENGTH
Realistic

FLAW is the direct opposite of STRENGTH

▲ SET-UP WANT sees its ultimate manifestation in TRIUMPH ▲▲

SET-UP WANT
Someone to watch movies with in the daytime

gets SET-UP WANT but there's a CATCH →
He's still married; she wears a wedding ring

tests the *FLAW*

POINT OF NO RETURN
Halley accepts his invitation to watch footage (24–25%: 0:25:00–0:26:07)

TRIUMPH
He kisses Halley. She tells him she's not ready, and he kisses her again (74–75%: 1:17:12–1:18:23)

fails to move toward *STRENGTH*

CLIMACTIC CHOICE
He proposes to Halley

worsens *FLAW*

fails to move toward *STRENGTH*

FINAL STEP
Tells Judah that his "fictional" protagonist should turn himself in

worsens *FLAW*

▶ ACT 1   25% ▶ ACT 2   75% ▶ ACT 3

Timeline not to scale.

Dallas Buyers Club

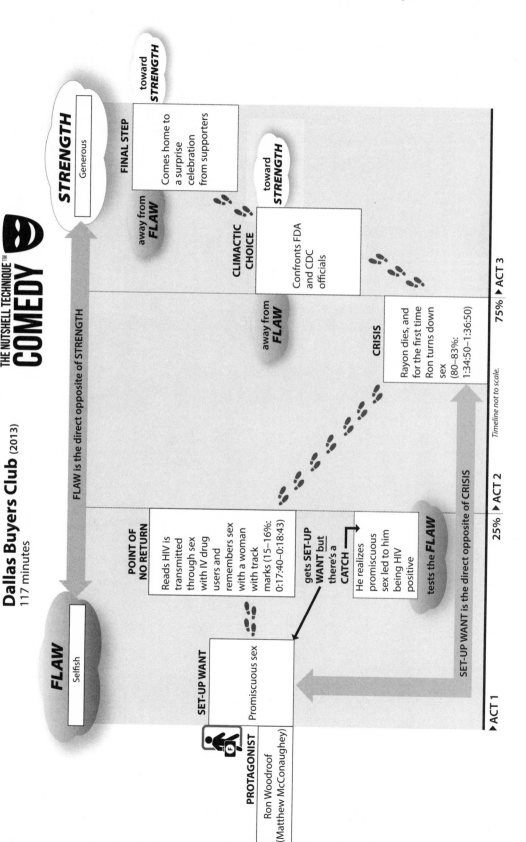

THE NUTSHELL TECHNIQUE™
COMEDY

Dallas Buyers Club (2013)
117 minutes

FLAW
Selfish

FLAW is the direct opposite of STRENGTH

STRENGTH
Generous

PROTAGONIST
Ron Woodroof (Matthew McConaughey)

SET-UP WANT
Promiscuous sex

POINT OF NO RETURN
Reads HIV is transmitted through sex with IV drug users and remembers sex with a woman with track marks (15–16%: 0:17:40–0:18:43)

gets SET-UP WANT but there's a **CATCH**
He realizes promiscuous sex led to him being HIV positive

tests the FLAW

SET-UP WANT is the direct opposite of CRISIS

CRISIS
Rayon dies, and for the first time Ron turns down sex (80–83%: 1:34:50–1:36:50)

away from **FLAW**

CLIMACTIC CHOICE
Confronts FDA and CDC officials

away from **FLAW**

FINAL STEP
Comes home to a surprise celebration from supporters

toward **STRENGTH**

toward **STRENGTH**

▶ ACT 1   25% ▶ ACT 2   *Timeline not to scale.*   75% ▶ ACT 3

Frozen

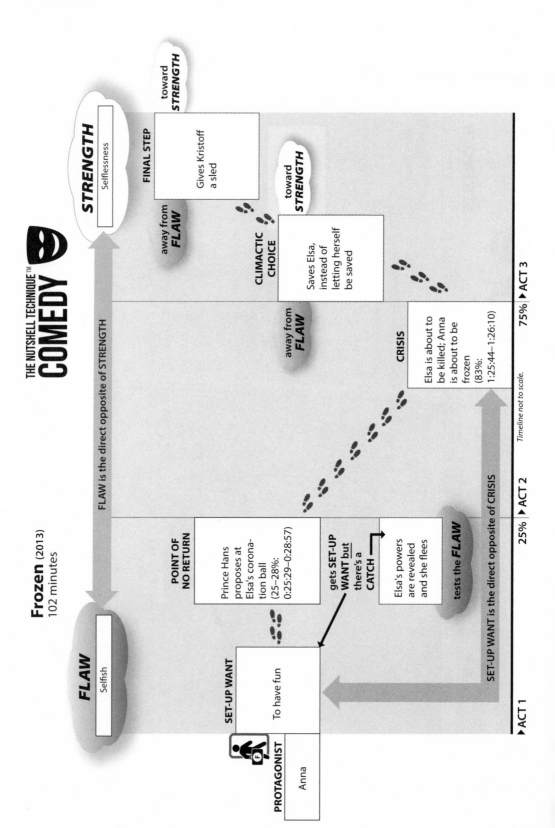

THE NUTSHELL TECHNIQUE™
COMEDY

Frozen (2013)
102 minutes

FLAW is the direct opposite of STRENGTH

FLAW — Selfish

STRENGTH — Selflessness

PROTAGONIST — Anna

SET-UP WANT — To have fun

POINT OF NO RETURN — Prince Hans proposes at Elsa's coronation ball (25–28%: 0:25:29–0:28:57)

gets **SET-UP WANT** but there's a CATCH — Elsa's powers are revealed and she flees

tests the **FLAW**

SET-UP WANT is the direct opposite of CRISIS

CRISIS — Elsa is about to be killed; Anna is about to be frozen (83%: 1:25:44–1:26:10)

away from **FLAW**

CLIMACTIC CHOICE — Saves Elsa, instead of letting herself be saved

toward **STRENGTH**

away from **FLAW**

FINAL STEP — Gives Kristoff a sled

toward **STRENGTH**

▶ ACT 1   25% ▶ ACT 2   75% ▶ ACT 3

Timeline not to scale.

The Godfather

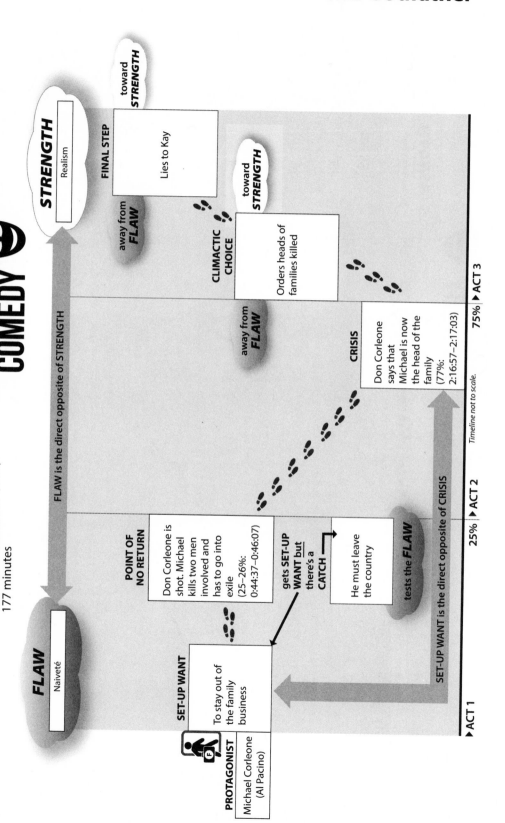

THE NUTSHELL TECHNIQUE™
COMEDY

The Godfather (1972)
177 minutes

STRENGTH
Realism

FLAW is the direct opposite of STRENGTH

FINAL STEP
away from **FLAW**
Lies to Kay
toward **STRENGTH**

CLIMACTIC CHOICE
away from **FLAW**
Orders heads of families killed
toward **STRENGTH**

FLAW
Naiveté

POINT OF NO RETURN
Don Corleone is shot. Michael kills two men involved and has to go into exile (25–26%: 0:44:37–0:46:07)

gets SET-UP WANT but there's a CATCH
He must leave the country

SET-UP WANT
To stay out of the family business

CRISIS
Don Corleone says that Michael is now the head of the family (77%: 2:16:57–2:17:03)

tests the **FLAW**

SET-UP WANT is the direct opposite of CRISIS

PROTAGONIST
Michael Corleone (Al Pacino)

▶ ACT 1   25% ▶ ACT 2   *Timeline not to scale.*   75% ▶ ACT 3

Groundhog Day

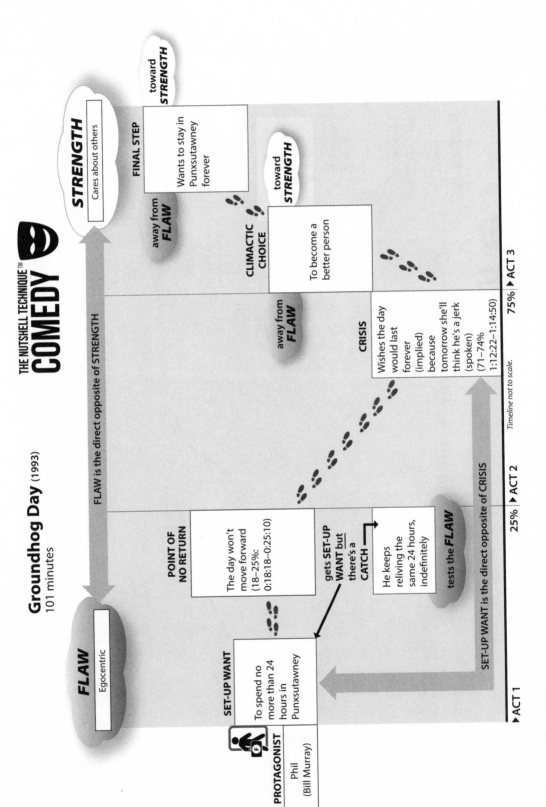

Groundhog Day (1993)
101 minutes

THE NUTSHELL TECHNIQUE™
COMEDY

FLAW
Egocentric

FLAW is the direct opposite of STRENGTH

STRENGTH
Cares about others

FINAL STEP

toward *STRENGTH*

Wants to stay in Punxsutawney forever

away from *FLAW*

CLIMACTIC CHOICE

To become a better person

toward *STRENGTH*

away from *FLAW*

CRISIS

Wishes the day would last forever (implied) because tomorrow she'll think he's a jerk (spoken)
(71–74%)
1:12:22–1:14:50)

POINT OF NO RETURN

The day won't move forward
(18–25%:
0:18:18–0:25:10)

gets SET-UP WANT but there's a **CATCH**

He keeps reliving the same 24 hours, indefinitely

tests the *FLAW*

SET-UP WANT

To spend no more than 24 hours in Punxsutawney

PROTAGONIST

Phil (Bill Murray)

SET-UP WANT is the direct opposite of CRISIS

▶ ACT 1

25% | ▶ ACT 2

75% | ▶ ACT 3

Timeline not to scale.

Juno

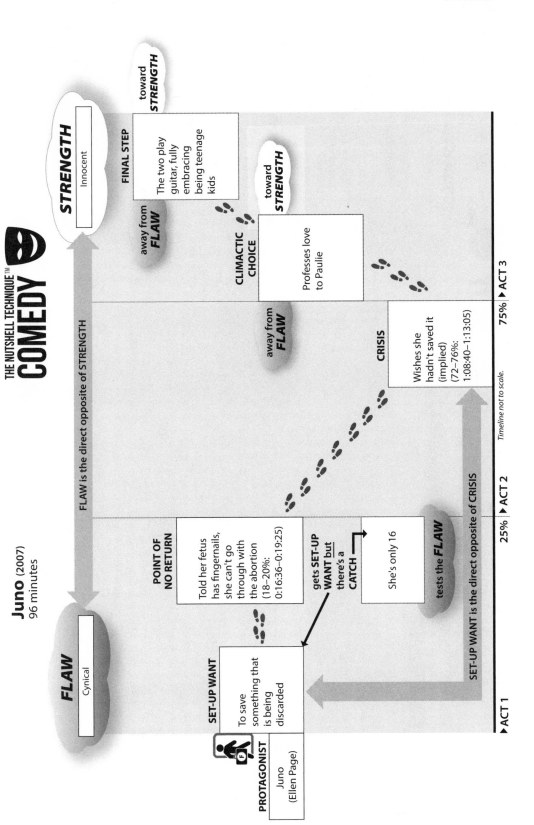

Juno (2007)
96 minutes

THE NUTSHELL TECHNIQUE™
COMEDY

FLAW
Cynical

FLAW is the direct opposite of STRENGTH

STRENGTH
Innocent

PROTAGONIST
Juno
(Ellen Page)

SET-UP WANT
To save something that is being discarded

gets **SET-UP WANT** but there's a **CATCH**

She's only 16

tests the **FLAW**

SET-UP WANT is the direct opposite of CRISIS

POINT OF NO RETURN
Told her fetus has fingernails, she can't go through with the abortion (18–20%: 0:16:36–0:19:25)

CRISIS
Wishes she hadn't saved it (implied) (72–76%: 1:08:40–1:13:05)

away from **FLAW**

CLIMACTIC CHOICE
Professes love to Paulie

toward **STRENGTH**

FINAL STEP
The two play guitar, fully embracing being teenage kids

away from **FLAW**

toward **STRENGTH**

▶ ACT 1   25% ▶ ACT 2   75% ▶ ACT 3

Timeline not to scale.

Little Miss Sunshine

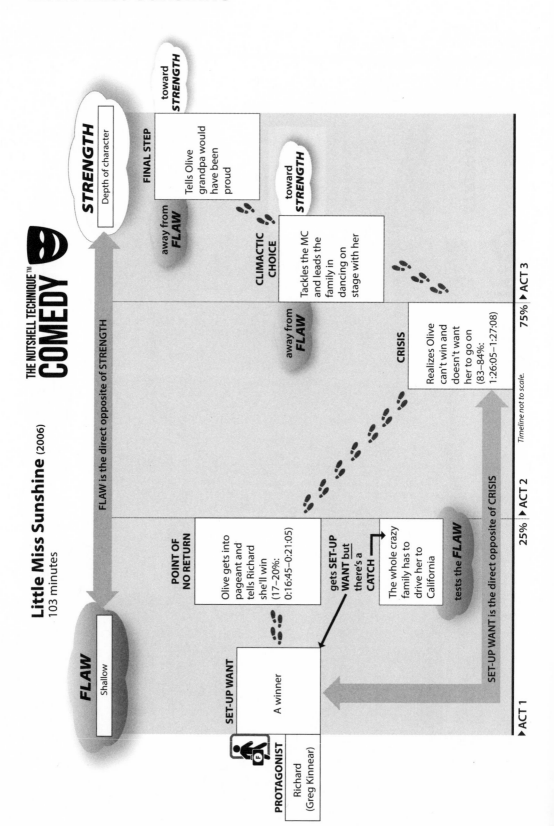

THE NUTSHELL TECHNIQUE™
COMEDY

Little Miss Sunshine (2006)
103 minutes

FLAW
Shallow

FLAW is the direct opposite of STRENGTH

STRENGTH
Depth of character

FINAL STEP
Tells Olive grandpa would have been proud

toward *STRENGTH*

away from *FLAW*

CLIMACTIC CHOICE
Tackles the MC and leads the family in dancing on stage with her

toward *STRENGTH*

away from *FLAW*

POINT OF NO RETURN
Olive gets into pageant and tells Richard she'll win
(17–20%: 0:16:45–0:21:05)

gets SET-UP WANT but there's a CATCH

The whole crazy family has to drive her to California

tests the *FLAW*

CRISIS
Realizes Olive can't win and doesn't want her to go on
(83–84%: 1:26:05–1:27:08)

SET-UP WANT
A winner

SET-UP WANT is the direct opposite of CRISIS

PROTAGONIST
Richard (Greg Kinnear)

▶ ACT 1   25% ▶ ACT 2   75% ▶ ACT 3

Timeline not to scale.

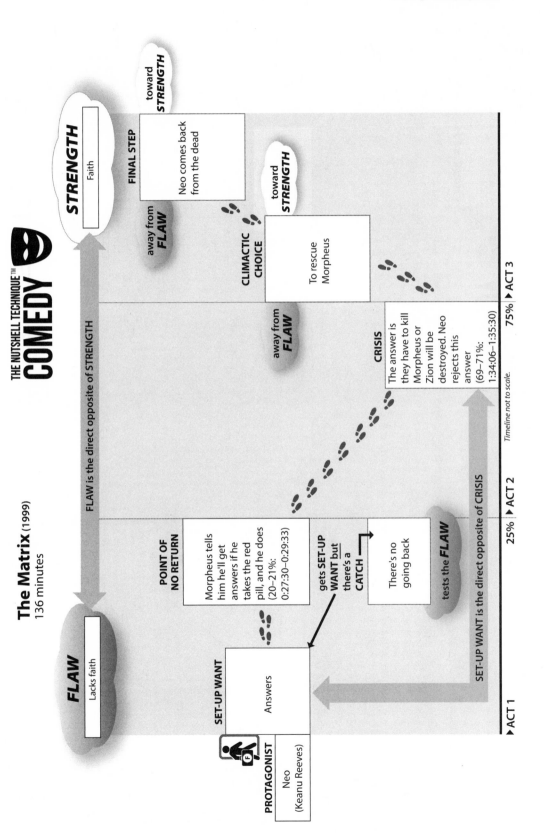

The Matrix

THE NUTSHELL TECHNIQUE™ COMEDY

The Matrix (1999)
136 minutes

STRENGTH
Faith

toward STRENGTH

FINAL STEP
Neo comes back from the dead

away from FLAW

CLIMACTIC CHOICE
To rescue Morpheus

toward STRENGTH

away from FLAW

CRISIS
The answer is they have to kill Morpheus or Zion will be destroyed. Neo rejects this answer (69–71%: 1:34:06–1:35:30)

FLAW is the direct opposite of STRENGTH

FLAW
Lacks faith

POINT OF NO RETURN
Morpheus tells him he'll get answers if he takes the red pill, and he does (20–21%: 0:27:30–0:29:33)

gets **SET-UP WANT** but there's a **CATCH**

There's no going back

tests the **FLAW**

SET-UP WANT
Answers

PROTAGONIST
Neo (Keanu Reeves)

SET-UP WANT is the direct opposite of CRISIS

Timeline not to scale.

▶ ACT 1   25% ▶ ACT 2   75% ▶ ACT 3

Memento

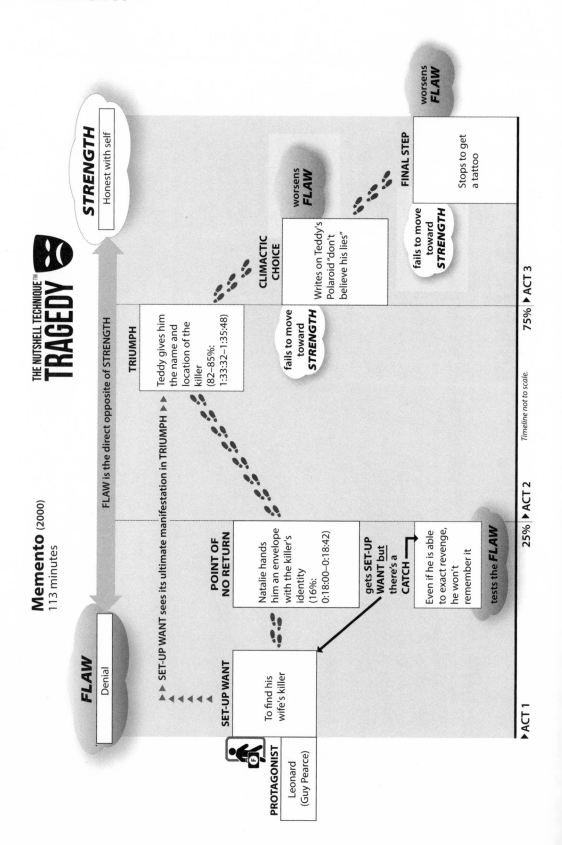

Memento (2000)
113 minutes

THE NUTSHELL TECHNIQUE™
TRAGEDY

FLAW is the direct opposite of STRENGTH

STRENGTH
Honest with self

FLAW
Denial

▲ SET-UP WANT sees its ultimate manifestation in TRIUMPH ▲

TRIUMPH
Teddy gives him the name and location of the killer (82–85%: 1:33:32–1:35:48)

CLIMACTIC CHOICE
Writes on Teddy's Polaroid "don't believe his lies"

worsens FLAW

fails to move toward STRENGTH

FINAL STEP
Stops to get a tattoo

worsens FLAW

fails to move toward STRENGTH

POINT OF NO RETURN
Natalie hands him an envelope with the killer's identity (16%: 0:18:00–0:18:42)

gets SET-UP WANT but there's a CATCH

Even if he is able to exact revenge, he won't remember it

tests the FLAW

SET-UP WANT
To find his wife's killer

PROTAGONIST
Leonard (Guy Pearce)

▶ ACT 1   25% ▶ ACT 2   75% ▶ ACT 3

Timeline not to scale.

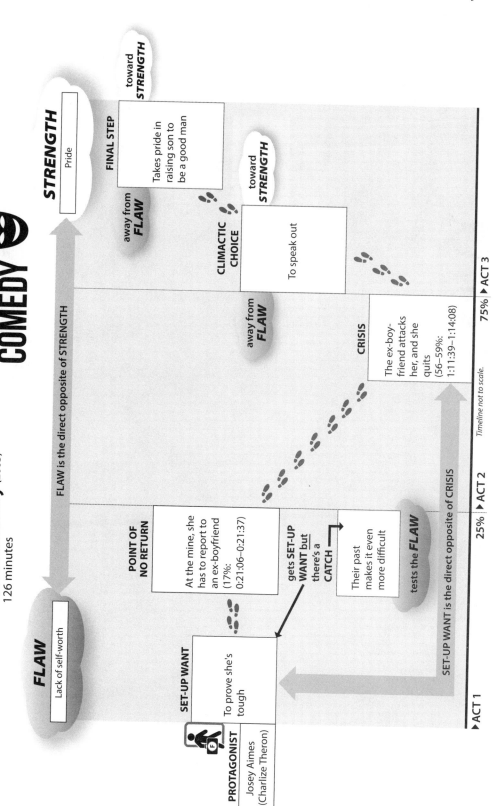

THE NUTSHELL TECHNIQUE™
COMEDY

North Country (2005)
126 minutes

PROTAGONIST
Josey Aimes (Charlize Theron)

SET-UP WANT
To prove she's tough

FLAW
Lack of self-worth

FLAW is the direct opposite of STRENGTH

STRENGTH
Pride

POINT OF NO RETURN
At the mine, she has to report to an ex-boyfriend (17%: 0:21:06–0:21:37)

gets SET-UP WANT but there's a CATCH
Their past makes it even more difficult

tests the FLAW

FINAL STEP
toward STRENGTH
Takes pride in raising son to be a good man

away from FLAW

CLIMACTIC CHOICE
toward STRENGTH
To speak out

away from FLAW

CRISIS
The ex-boyfriend attacks her, and she quits (56–59%: 1:11:39–1:14:08)

SET-UP WANT is the direct opposite of CRISIS

▶ ACT 1   25% ▶ ACT 2   *Timeline not to scale.*   75% ▶ ACT 3

Pulp Fiction

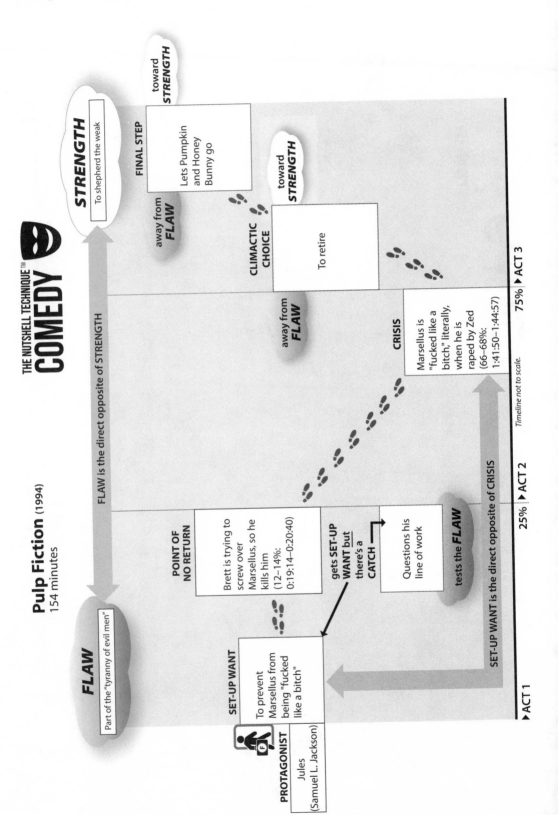

THE NUTSHELL TECHNIQUE™
COMEDY

Pulp Fiction (1994)
154 minutes

STRENGTH
To shepherd the weak

FLAW is the direct opposite of STRENGTH

FLAW
Part of the "tyranny of evil men"

FINAL STEP
toward *STRENGTH*

Lets Pumpkin and Honey Bunny go

away from *FLAW*

CLIMACTIC CHOICE
toward *STRENGTH*

To retire

away from *FLAW*

CRISIS
Marsellus is "fucked like a bitch," literally, when he is raped by Zed (66–68%: 1:41:50–1:44:57)

Timeline not to scale.

POINT OF NO RETURN
Brett is trying to screw over Marsellus, so he kills him (12–14%: 0:19:14–0:20:40)

gets SET-UP WANT but there's a **CATCH**

Questions his line of work

tests the FLAW

SET-UP WANT is the direct opposite of CRISIS

SET-UP WANT
To prevent Marsellus from being "fucked like a bitch"

PROTAGONIST
Jules (Samuel L. Jackson)

▶ ACT 1   25% ▶ ACT 2   75% ▶ ACT 3

Silver Linings Playbook

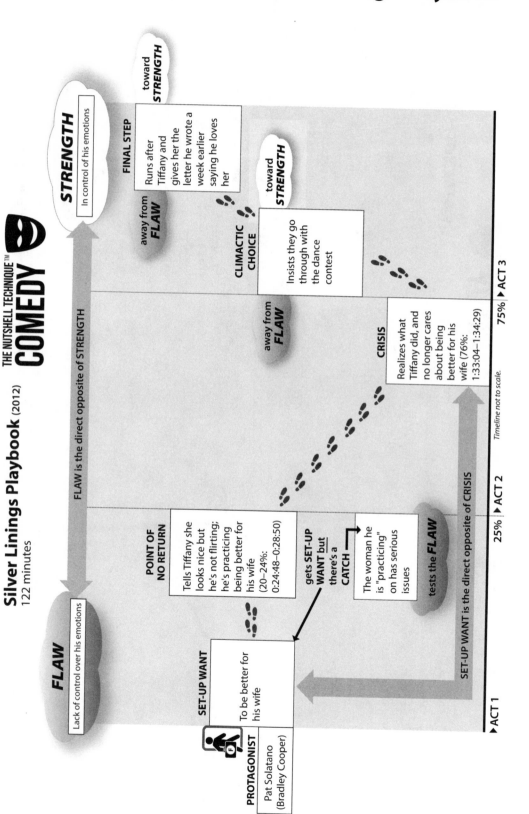

Silver Linings Playbook (2012)
122 minutes

THE NUTSHELL TECHNIQUE™
COMEDY

FLAW
Lack of control over his emotions

FLAW is the direct opposite of STRENGTH

STRENGTH
In control of his emotions

FINAL STEP

away from **FLAW**

toward **STRENGTH**

Runs after Tiffany and gives her the letter he wrote a week earlier saying he loves her

CLIMACTIC CHOICE

away from **FLAW**

toward **STRENGTH**

Insists they go through with the dance contest

CRISIS

Realizes what Tiffany did, and no longer cares about being better for his wife (76%: 1:33:04–1:34:29)

POINT OF NO RETURN

Tells Tiffany she looks nice but he's not flirting; he's practicing being better for his wife (20–24%: 0:24:48–0:28:50)

gets **SET-UP WANT** but there's a **CATCH**

The woman he is "practicing" on has serious issues

tests the **FLAW**

SET-UP WANT

To be better for his wife

PROTAGONIST

Pat Solatano (Bradley Cooper)

SET-UP WANT is the direct opposite of CRISIS

▶ ACT 1   25% ▶ ACT 2   *Timeline not to scale.*   75% ▶ ACT 3

The Sixth Sense

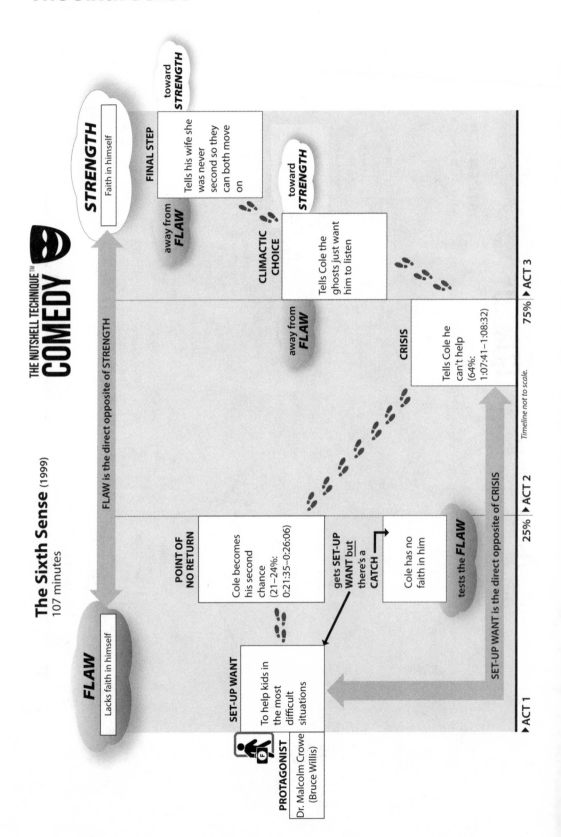

The Sixth Sense (1999)
107 minutes

THE NUTSHELL TECHNIQUE™
COMEDY

PROTAGONIST
Dr. Malcolm Crowe (Bruce Willis)

FLAW
Lacks faith in himself

FLAW is the direct opposite of STRENGTH

STRENGTH
Faith in himself

SET-UP WANT
To help kids in the most difficult situations

gets SET-UP WANT but there's a CATCH
Cole has no faith in him

POINT OF NO RETURN
Cole becomes his second chance (21–24%: 0:21:35–0:26:06)

tests the **FLAW**

SET-UP WANT is the direct opposite of CRISIS

CRISIS
Tells Cole he can't help (64%: 1:07:41–1:08:32)

away from **FLAW**

CLIMACTIC CHOICE
Tells Cole the ghosts just want him to listen

toward **STRENGTH**

away from **FLAW**

FINAL STEP
Tells his wife she was never second so they can both move on

toward **STRENGTH**

► ACT 1   25% ► ACT 2   75% ► ACT 3

Timeline not to scale.

The Social Network

The Social Network (2010)
120 minutes

THE NUTSHELL TECHNIQUE™
TRAGEDY

PROTAGONIST
Mark Zuckerberg (Jesse Eisenberg)

STRENGTH
Humility

FLAW
Hubris

FLAW is the direct opposite of STRENGTH

▶▶ SET-UP WANT sees its ultimate manifestation in TRIUMPH ▶▶

SET-UP WANT
To get into a final club

POINT OF NO RETURN
In a final club, he gets the inspiration for Facebook (18–23%: 0:22:21–0:27:29)

gets SET-UP WANT but there's a CATCH
His idea could be seen as similar to the Winklevosses'

tests the *FLAW*

TRIUMPH
He's the CEO of his own "final club" with a million members (84%: 1:41:10–1:41:15)

fails to move toward *STRENGTH*

CLIMACTIC CHOICE
Cheats his best friend in the new deal

worsens *FLAW*

fails to move toward *STRENGTH*

FINAL STEP
He sends his ex-girlfriend a Friend Request and hits Refresh over and over

worsens *FLAW*

▶ ACT 1   25% ▶ ACT 2   75% ▶ ACT 3

Timeline not to scale.

Sunset Blvd.

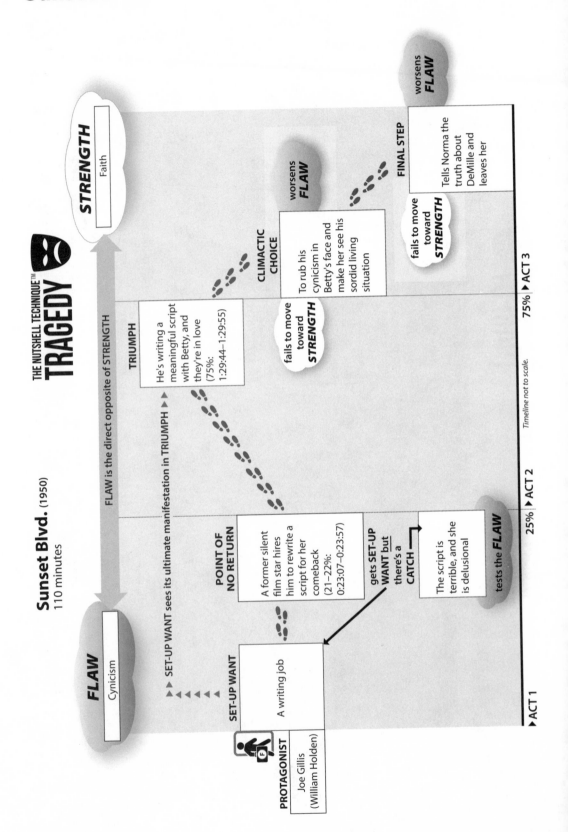

Sunset Blvd. (1950)
110 minutes

THE NUTSHELL TECHNIQUE™
TRAGEDY

FLAW
Cynicism

FLAW is the direct opposite of STRENGTH

STRENGTH
Faith

▶▶ SET-UP WANT sees its ultimate manifestation in TRIUMPH ▶▶

PROTAGONIST
Joe Gillis
(William Holden)

SET-UP WANT
A writing job

POINT OF NO RETURN
A former silent film star hires him to rewrite a script for her comeback (21–22%: 0:23:07–0:23:57)

gets SET-UP WANT but there's a CATCH

The script is terrible, and she is delusional

tests the **FLAW**

TRIUMPH
He's writing a meaningful script with Betty, and they're in love (75%: 1:29:44–1:29:55)

fails to move toward **STRENGTH**

CLIMACTIC CHOICE
To rub his cynicism in Betty's face and make her see his sordid living situation

worsens **FLAW**

fails to move toward **STRENGTH**

FINAL STEP
Tells Norma the truth about DeMille and leaves her

worsens **FLAW**

▶ ACT 1   25% ▶ ACT 2   75% ▶ ACT 3

Timeline not to scale.

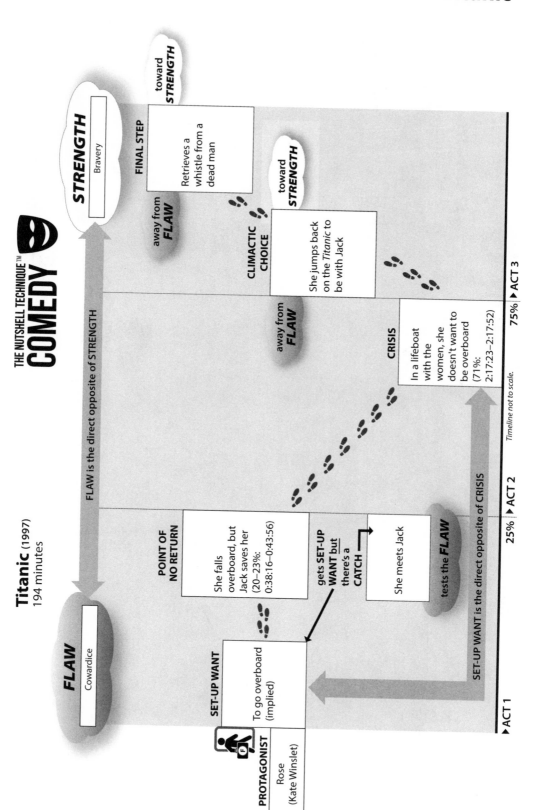

Titanic

THE NUTSHELL TECHNIQUE™
COMEDY

Titanic (1997)
194 minutes

FLAW
Cowardice

FLAW is the direct opposite of STRENGTH

STRENGTH
Bravery

FINAL STEP
toward **STRENGTH**

Retrieves a whistle from a dead man

away from **FLAW**

CLIMACTIC CHOICE
toward **STRENGTH**

She jumps back on the *Titanic* to be with Jack

away from **FLAW**

CRISIS
In a lifeboat with the women, she doesn't want to be overboard (71%: 2:17:23–2:17:52)

PROTAGONIST
Rose (Kate Winslet)

SET-UP WANT
To go overboard (implied)

gets SET-UP WANT but there's a CATCH

She meets Jack

POINT OF NO RETURN
She falls overboard, but Jack saves her (20–23%: 0:38:16–0:43:56)

tests the **FLAW**

SET-UP WANT is the direct opposite of CRISIS

▶ ACT 1   25% ▶ ACT 2   *Timeline not to scale.*   75% ▶ ACT 3

Tootsie

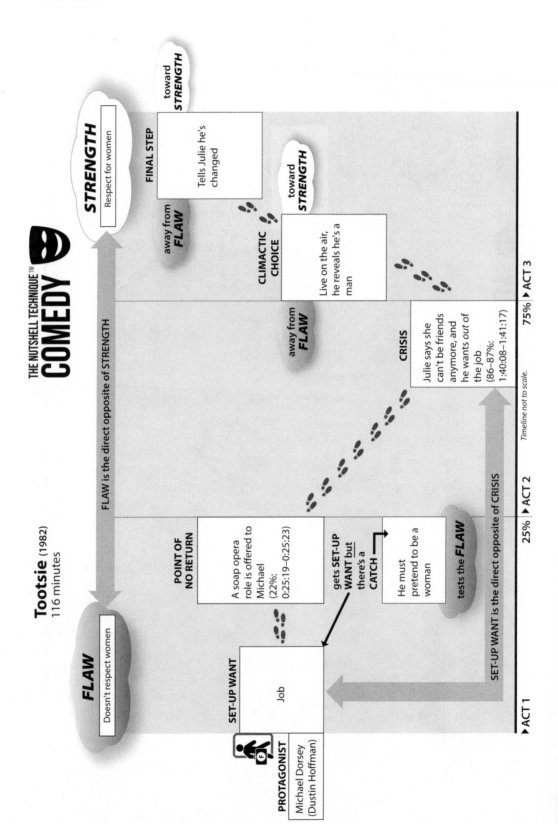

THE NUTSHELL TECHNIQUE™
COMEDY

Tootsie (1982)
116 minutes

STRENGTH
Respect for women

FLAW
Doesn't respect women

FLAW is the direct opposite of STRENGTH

PROTAGONIST
Michael Dorsey
(Dustin Hoffman)

SET-UP WANT
Job

SET-UP WANT is the direct opposite of CRISIS

POINT OF NO RETURN
A soap opera role is offered to Michael (22%: 0:25:19–0:25:23)

gets SET-UP WANT but there's a CATCH

He must pretend to be a woman

tests the FLAW

CRISIS
Julie says she can't be friends anymore, and he wants out of the job (86–87%: 1:40:08–1:41:17)

CLIMACTIC CHOICE
Live on the air, he reveals he's a man

away from FLAW

toward STRENGTH

FINAL STEP
Tells Julie he's changed

away from FLAW

toward STRENGTH

▶ ACT 1   25% ▶ ACT 2   75% ▶ ACT 3

Timeline not to scale.

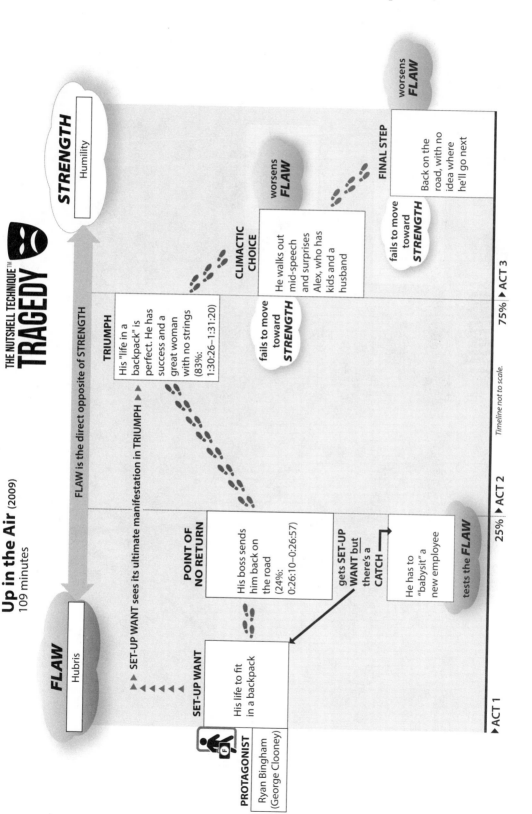

Up in the Air

THE NUTSHELL TECHNIQUE™
TRAGEDY

Up in the Air (2009)
109 minutes

PROTAGONIST
Ryan Bingham (George Clooney)

FLAW
Hubris

STRENGTH
Humility

FLAW is the direct opposite of STRENGTH

▶ SET-UP WANT sees its ultimate manifestation in TRIUMPH ▶

SET-UP WANT
His life to fit in a backpack

gets SET-UP WANT but there's a CATCH

He has to "babysit" a new employee

tests the FLAW

POINT OF NO RETURN
His boss sends him back on the road (24%: 0:26:10–0:26:57)

TRIUMPH
His "life in a backpack" is perfect. He has success and a great woman with no strings (83%: 1:30:26–1:31:20)

fails to move toward STRENGTH

CLIMACTIC CHOICE
He walks out mid-speech and surprises Alex, who has kids and a husband

worsens FLAW

fails to move toward STRENGTH

FINAL STEP
Back on the road, with no idea where he'll go next

worsens FLAW

▶ ACT 1   25% ▶ ACT 2   75% ▶ ACT 3

Timeline not to scale.

The Usual Suspects

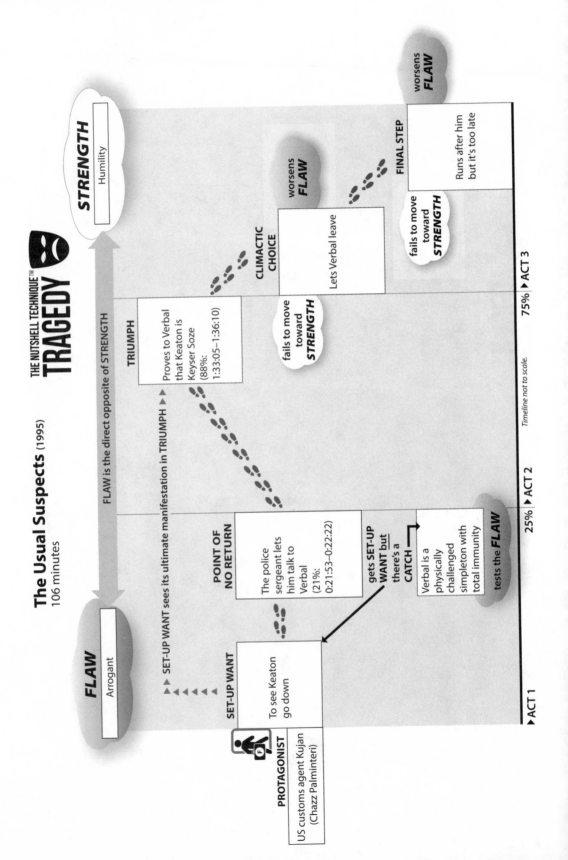

The Usual Suspects (1995)
106 minutes

THE NUTSHELL TECHNIQUE™
TRAGEDY

FLAW is the direct opposite of STRENGTH

▶▶ SET-UP WANT sees its ultimate manifestation in TRIUMPH ▶▶

FLAW
Arrogant

STRENGTH
Humility

PROTAGONIST
US customs agent Kujan (Chazz Palminteri)

SET-UP WANT
To see Keaton go down

gets **SET-UP WANT** but there's a **CATCH**

Verbal is a physically challenged simpleton with total immunity

tests the **FLAW**

POINT OF NO RETURN
The police sergeant lets him talk to Verbal
(21%: 0:21:53–0:22:22)

TRIUMPH
Proves to Verbal that Keaton is Keyser Soze
(88%: 1:33:05–1:36:10)

fails to move toward **STRENGTH**

CLIMACTIC CHOICE
Lets Verbal leave

worsens **FLAW**

fails to move toward **STRENGTH**

FINAL STEP
Runs after him but it's too late

worsens **FLAW**

▶ ACT 1   25% ▶ ACT 2   75% ▶ ACT 3

Timeline not to scale.

THE NUTSHELL TECHNIQUE™
COMEDY

Witness (1985)
112 minutes

FLAW

Loner

FLAW is the direct opposite of STRENGTH

STRENGTH

Values community

FINAL STEP

To go back to his own community and make room for Rachel's suitor, who belongs

toward STRENGTH

away from FLAW

CLIMACTIC CHOICE

To face him the Amish way, as a group all bearing witness

toward STRENGTH

away from FLAW

POINT OF NO RETURN

The boy identifies a cop as the killer, Book tells his mentor, and the killer cop tries to kill Book (25–29%: 0:27:50–0:32:13)

CRISIS

The killer finds him (81–84%: 1:31:00–1:34:17)

SET-UP WANT

To find the killer

gets SET-UP WANT <u>but</u> there's a **CATCH**

His mentor is in on the conspiracy

tests the **FLAW**

PROTAGONIST

John Book (Harrison Ford)

SET-UP WANT is the direct opposite of CRISIS

▶ ACT 1   25% ▶ ACT 2   75% ▶ ACT 3

Timeline not to scale.

Film Nutshell Commentary

ANNIE HALL

The American Film Institute ranks *Annie Hall* the #4 comedy of all time, but, in fact, it is, structurally speaking, a perfect tragedy.

In his first scene, protagonist Alvy Singer (Woody Allen) addresses the camera, saying that he's not over his breakup with Annie, and he keeps playing their relationship over in his head, trying to figure out where they went wrong. That's what he says, but I don't think it's a reach to say that what he really wants is to prove to himself they shouldn't have broken up, because he doesn't want to be broken up. And that's really what you're doing when you obsess about where a relationship went wrong.

The rest of Act 1 jumps back and forth in time until at the POINT OF NO RETURN he goes to the moment when he and Annie first met at a tennis game and she gave him a ride home (26–30%: 0:24:30–0:27:38). This first meeting is promising enough that he has his SET-UP WANT: he's proven to himself that they shouldn't have broken up. The CATCH, that he <u>doesn't want to belong to a club that would have him as a member</u>, is a sentiment mentioned in his opening monologue. The Groucho Marx joke, he tells us then, sums up his relationships with women. In other words, if Annie loves him, he won't be able to love her.

At his TRIUMPH (at 65%: 1:00:23–1:00:29), <u>they got back together and she had them promise they'll never break up again</u>. Eventually, however, his tragic FLAW that he's <u>self-absorbed</u> gets in the way. After a singing concert of hers, a famous producer tells her he'd like to work with her and invites them to a party. Selfishly not wanting to go, Alvy begs them off with that lamest of excuses: "Remember, we have that thing."

THE BIG LEBOWSKI

I wanted to include one Coen brothers film, and *The Big Lebowski* is their most recent film that I could Nutshell. Their early films, like *Blood Simple* and *Raising Arizona*, do Nutshell, but after that, it gets spotty. And then there's *Fargo*. Not only can I not Nutshell it, I can't find the act breaks (and I can always at least find the act breaks). I think *Fargo* is a great film. I really like the Coen brothers and their stories. I can't accept that they have no structure, but then again, I am a structuralist. Movies aren't entertaining or moving or inspiring by accident. Usually they are one or more of these things because they are well structured. Lack of structure doesn't equal originality. Lack of structure means haphazard events that happen for no rhyme or reason, like in life. But well-told stories aren't life. The Coen brothers films are well made—so well made, I'm convinced that somewhere along the way they invented a structuring technique all their own.

BRAVEHEART

Yes, I'm well aware that the FLAW of <u>rage</u> and the STRENGTH of <u>courage</u> aren't opposites. Also William still has plenty of rage in Act 3, and he's pretty darn brave in Acts 1 and 2. But he does go through an Act 3 transformation from someone with a warrior's courage to someone with the almost superhuman courage to not cave under torture. His death is his final act of rebellion against the British. He knows it will inspire his countrymen to eventually win their freedom. To William Wallace, it is a happy ending.

FROZEN

I've noticed that in animated family films, the CRISIS is often some kind of threat of death. Which is kind of the opposite of everything (e.g., "to have fun," "to play," "to eat ice cream"), but in reality it's the opposite of "no threat of death." In my opinion having a CRISIS that is a threat of death to simply negate any SET-UP WANT is weak. It lacks the ironic power of a true reversal.

THE GODFATHER

There are a few irregularities with this Nutshell. Don Vito Corleone is shot at 22–26% of the running time (at 0:44:37–0:46:07). This leads to Michael killing two men who were involved at 1:29:18, which then leads to him having to go live in Sicily in exile. The POINT OF NO RETURN is supposed to bring an immediate CATCH, but in this case the CATCH, <u>he must leave the country</u>, doesn't happen until almost 45 minutes after the POINT OF NO RETURN.

His CRISIS (<u>Don Corleone says that Michael is now the head of the</u>

family) isn't his lowest moment, as it is supposed to be. But it does meet the other requirement of the CRISIS, the one that gives the story irony: it's the opposite of his SET-UP WANT, to stay out of the family business.

In all the Film Nutshells in this book except this one, the FLAW-to-STRENGTH transformation (or failure to transform in tragedy) reveals universal morals with which most people would agree. For example, most people would agree it's a good thing that *Tootsie*'s Michael learns in the end the STRENGTH of respect for women. In *The Godfather*, however, most people wouldn't identify Michael's transformation from the FLAW of naiveté to the STRENGTH of realism as a good thing. He is not a better person because of it, but actually a worse one. That realism is a STRENGTH is relative to him and the world of the film, and not a universal truth, unlike in all the other Film Nutshells in this book.

GROUNDHOG DAY

I love the delicious irony of a man trapped repeating the same day over and over wishing, in his CRISIS, that the day would last forever. But apparently the filmmakers found this too heavy-handed because Phil doesn't actually say this. He comes very close. He and Rita have just had this great day together. And he says that he hates that tomorrow she won't remember any of this and will think he's a jerk again. He clearly wishes the day would last forever so these things won't happen. But he doesn't say it. I think it would have been an even better film if he had. Irony is a powerful tool for the screenwriter.

JUNO

Leaving the note for Vanessa doesn't count as the CLIMACTIC CHOICE because the contents of the note aren't revealed to the audience until the very end. The CLIMACTIC CHOICE is central to the Climax, so the audience needs to know what it is as it is happening.

PULP FICTION

See discussion regarding the CATCH in Chapter 15, "Nonlinear Screenplays."

NOTES

CHAPTER 1

1. Aristotle, *Aristotle: The Poetics. "Longinus": On the Sublime. Demetrius: On Style* (London: William Heinemann; Cambridge, MA: Harvard University Press, 1939), 47. There is considerable debate about whether the translation of the word "hamartia" (ancient Greek: ἁμαρτία), here translated as "flaw," is accurate. Regardless of what the original author intended, defining the tragic protagonist's change of fortune from good to bad as being due to their own flaw has become a very useful distinction used by many an instructor of dramatic structure.

2. Only the first part of *The Poetics*, which focuses mainly on tragedy, survives. The lost second part deals with comedy. In the extant *Poetics*, Aristotle said that tragedies should have sad endings because the protagonist is brought down by their own flaw, and comedies should have happy endings (ibid., 48) but he did not say the protagonist overcomes a flaw in a comedy. I, and others, have extrapolated that if in a tragedy the protagonist has a sad ending because they are brought down by a flaw, then in a comedy the protagonist has a happy ending because they overcome a flaw. Regardless of Aristotle's original intentions, dividing all drama into either comedies or tragedies defined like this is commonplace among teachers of dramatic structure.

3. Ibid., 37, 39.

4. Ibid., 39.

5. Ibid., 41.

6. Ibid., 69.

CHAPTER 6

1. M. Night Shyamalan, *The Sixth Sense*. Final shooting script, November 2, 1998. (Held by the Writers Guild Foundation's Shavelson-Webb Library.)

CHAPTER 7

1. Held by the Writers Guild Foundation's Shavelson-Webb Library.

2. Beat is one of those annoying words in film that is used to mean a couple of completely different things. The sense of beat I'm using, meaning an event that may take place over multiple scene headers before it is complete, is the same kind of beat a beat sheet refers to. A beat sheet is a list of all the events in the screenplay that a screenwriter may write up when developing a story and use as a road map to organize the plot before actually writing the script. This should not be confused with the word beat as used mostly by actors and directors to refer to a much smaller action: one exchange of action and reaction within a single scene. Yet another use of the word beat is seen in screenplay parentheticals: (beat). This last usage is a suggestion for the actor speaking to take a pause.

3. Tony Gilroy, *The Bourne Identity*. Film script, revised through February 15, 2001. (Held by the Academy of Motion Picture Arts and Sciences Margaret Herrick Library.)

4. Stuart Beattie, *Collateral*. Film script, revised through January 20, 2004. (Held by the Academy of Motion Picture Arts and Sciences Margaret Herrick Library.)

CHAPTER 9

1. *On Story*. Television series, Episode 201: "Creating Memorable Characters," May 26, 2012.

2. Clara Bingham and Laura Leedy Gansler, *Class Action: The Story of Lois Jenson and the Landmark Case That Changed Sexual Harassment Law* (New York: Doubleday, 2002).

3. Ibid.

CHAPTER 12

1. This definition is often attributed to Aristotle, who actually said, more generally, that great plots are comprised of incidents that are inevitable and unexpected. Aristotle, *Aristotle: The Poetics. "Longinus": On the Sublime. Demetrius: On Style* (London: William Heinemann; Cambridge, MA: Harvard University Press, 1939), 39.

CHAPTER 15

1. *Sunset Blvd.* and *Titanic* both tell the majority of their respective stories in a central flashback. *The Usual Suspects* similarly relates the majority of the dramatic story in Verbal's telling of what happened. These three films' use of a framing central flashback is not typically referred to as nonlinear. Certainly the films defined in Chapter 15 as nonlinear go much further in bending the representation of time than a mere framing flashback.

Film characters are in **boldface font** and alphabetized by first name; charts, film stills, and forms are denoted by f following the page number.